Driving Theory Test Questions

Driving Theory Test Questions

Published by
The British School of
Motoring Ltd in
association with
Virgin Publishing

First published in the UK in 1996 by
The British School of Motoring Ltd
81/87 Hartfield Road
Wimbledon
LONDON SW19 3TJ

Second reprint 1996

ISBN 0 7535 0000 0

Design, typesetting and reprographics by Prima Creative Services
Printed and bound in Italy by Rotolito Lombarda S.p.A., Milan

Contents

Foreword

Driving is an enjoyable and valuable life skill which is why every year nearly a million new learner drivers take to the road, each one of them with one clear aim. This aim is almost certainly the same as yours – to gain their full driving licence.

There is no substitute for practical experience when learning to drive. The best way to gain this is by taking lessons with a good professional driving instructor who uses the most up-to-date teaching techniques in a modern, dual-controlled car.

However, it has always been equally important to prepare for your driving lessons and, since the introduction of the Theory Test, this is doubly true.

Driving Theory Test Questions contains the official Driving Standards Agency questions which are currently published and which may be included in the actual examination.

This book is an ideal study aid which allows you to test and revise your knowledge. It has been designed for use in conjunction with its companion volumes, *Pass Your Driving Theory Test* and *Pass Your Driving Test.*

Driving Theory Test Questions allows you to check your level of knowledge by presenting you with real examination questions. The questions are set out under topic headings, and as you work through each section you will prove to yourself that you not only understand what you have learnt, but can demonstrate this by answering the question correctly.

In doing so, you will gradually boost your confidence and thereby recognise when you are ready to take and pass your Theory Test.

Your driving instructor will help you to plan your studies and ensure that you fully understand why the knowledge you acquire is essential to keep you safe on the road, as well as to take you past that first all important hurdle of passing your Theory Test.

There are no short cuts to becoming a safe and competent motorist, but that does not mean that you cannot enjoy yourself while learning.

Driving Theory Test Questions and its companion volumes, will, I hope, bring the Theory Test alive and make it relevant, and at the same time it should also help you develop your driving skills.

In over 85 years of teaching people to drive, BSM instructors have helped millions of people pass their driving test. In my view, *Driving Theory Test Questions* complete the best set of books available to help you make the most of your driving lessons and ensure that you prepare for both the theory and practical parts of your driving test in a structured and positive way.

Keith Cameron
Road Safety Adviser

Keith Cameron is one of Britain's leading authorities on motoring and driver education. He has held a number of senior positions within the Department of Transport; up to March 1992 he was Chief Driving Examiner with responsibility for all UK driving tests.

Introduction

The driving test was first introduced to the UK back in 1935. Since that time millions of people have passed the driving test and gained their motoring freedom, many taught by BSM instructors. Despite the substantial increase in road traffic, the driving test has hardly changed in all that time – at least until the last few years. Reverse parking was introduced as a practical test exercise in 1991, and in 1995 the decision was made to bring in a separate written test.

Most of Europe has already been operating a separate theory test for some time. The new British test has been developed to satisfy European Community Regulations and to bring us more into line with our European counterparts.

The Theory Test is now here to stay and in order to become a qualified driver you must now pass the theory as well as the practical driving test.

Driving Theory Test Questions contains the official Driving Standards Agency questions which are currently published and which may be included in the actual examination. That means there are a lot of questions in this book, but when you take your Theory Test, you won't be expected to answer all of them! Your paper will only have 35 questions for you to answer.

I am sure your main aim is to pass the Theory Test. Nevertheless, I strongly urge you to do more than simply attempt to learn the answers parrot fashion. Not only will you find such a method of learning very tedious, you will also miss out on the chance to understand the significance of the information you are learning and make use of it when you practise with your instructor.

The list on the opposite page may seem daunting, but you can be completely confident that this book and its companion volumes, *Pass Your Driving Theory Test* and *Pass Your Driving Test*, cover each of the topic areas in detail.

Car and Motorcycle Theory Test Topics

Before each heading below, you will see the code S1, S2, S3 or S4. This indicates in which of the four sections of *Pass Your Driving Theory Test* you will find the topic covered.

MANDATORY TOPICS

S1 – Importance of alertness
Consideration, anticipation, observation, awareness, distraction, boredom.

S1 – Attitudes to other road users
Consideration, close following, courtesy, priority.

S1 – Knowledge of safe distances between vehicles, braking distances etc. (Conditions)
Safety margins and effect of bad weather and road surface conditions, visibility.

S1 – Impairment
Knowledge of reaction times and effects on driving behaviour of alcohol, fatigue, medication, drugs, stress, ill-health, ageing, sensory impairment (including eyesight).

S1 – Perception
Information processing, attention, scanning, identification of hazards, time to detect hazards, fixation, interpretation.

S1 – Judgement and decision-making
Appropriate action, interpretation, reaction time, speed, distance.

S2 – Risk factors associated with different road users
Children, pedestrians, disabled people, cyclists, elderly drivers, motorcyclists, new drivers/lack of traffic experience.

S2 – Risk factors associated with different road conditions
Own vehicle handling. Effects of: weather, road conditions, time of day (darkness), lighting, traffic calming, speed.

S2 – Behaviour in an accident
Rules on how to behave in case of an accident. Use of first aid kit and other first aid precautions, setting warning device and raising alarm, police reporting procedures, witness responsibilities, regulations.

S3 – Characteristics and statutory requirements of different types of roads
- Limitations on motorways: speed limits, lane discipline, stopping, lighting.
- Limitations on other types of road: speed limits, parking, clearways, lighting.

S3 – Road signs and traffic regulations
Road traffic regulations regarding road signs, markings, signals, rights of way and speed limits.

S4 – Administrative documents
Rules on administrative documents required for use of vehicles.

S4 – Safety factors relating to the vehicle and persons carried
Vehicle loading, stability, towing, regulations.

OPTIONAL TOPICS (Select one)

S4 – Mechanical aspects
How to detect the most common mechanical faults, defects that can affect safety, understanding of implications.

S4 – Vehicle safety equipment
Use of safety equipment (seat belts etc).

S4 – The environment
Rules on vehicle use in relation to the environment, emissions, fuel consumption, pollution (including noise), regulations.

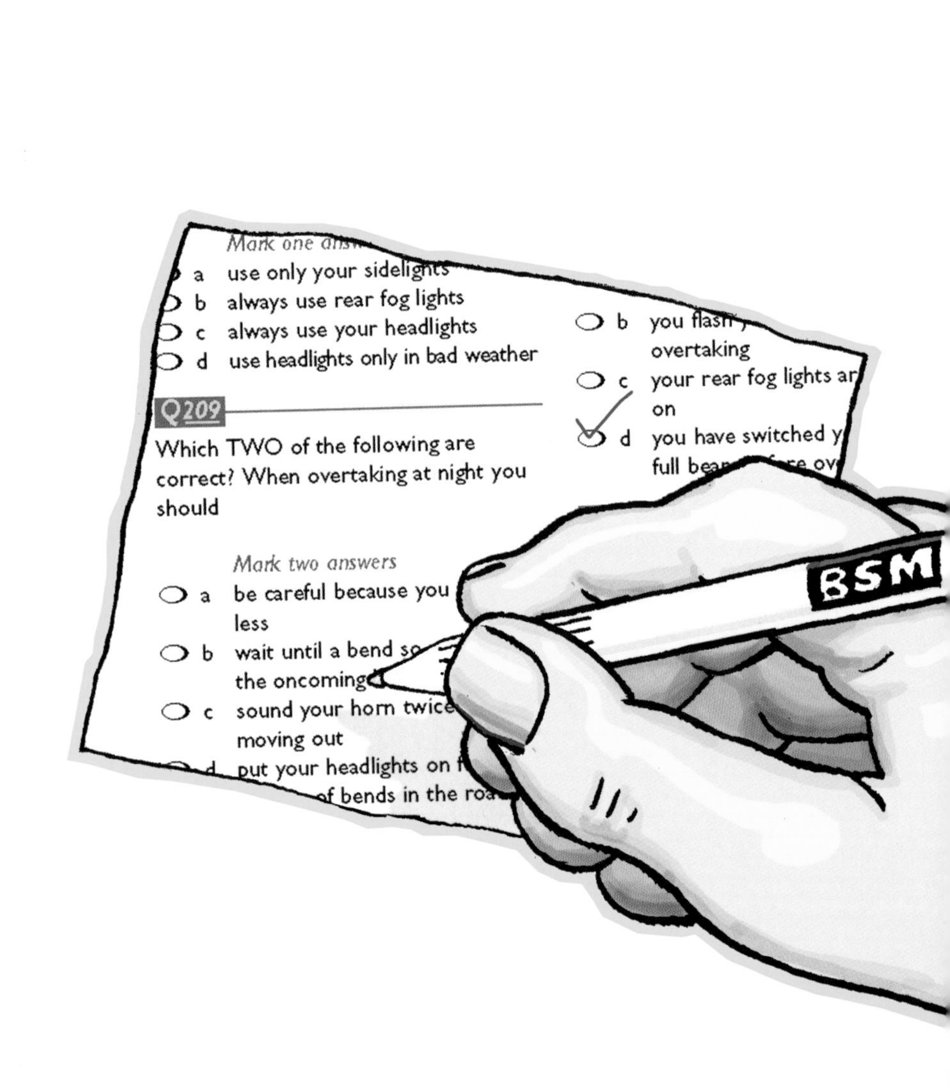

Mark one
a use only your sidelights
b always use rear fog lights
c always use your headlights
d use headlights only in bad weather
Q209
Which TWO of the following are correct? When overtaking at night you should
Mark two answers
a be careful because you
less
b wait until a bend
the oncoming
c sound your horn twice
moving out
d put your headlights on
of bends in the
b you
overtaking
c your rear fog lights
on
d you have switched
full
BSM

Alertness

Q001

To move off safely from a parked position you should

Mark one answer

- ❍ a signal if other drivers will need to slow down
- ❍ b NOT look round if there is a parked vehicle close in front of you
- ❍ c use your mirrors and look round for a final check
- ❍ d give a hand signal as well as using your indicators

Q002

You are driving a vehicle fitted with a hand telephone. To answer the telephone you MUST

Mark one answer

- ❍ a reduce your speed
- ❍ b find a safe place to stop
- ❍ c steer the car with one hand
- ❍ d be particularly careful at junctions

Q003

You want to move off from a parked position. The road is busy with traffic passing from behind. You should

Mark one answer

- ❍ a give a signal and move away as soon as someone flashes you
- ❍ b wait without signalling for a safe gap in the traffic
- ❍ c signal while waiting for a gap in the traffic
- ❍ d edge your way into the traffic until someone gives way

Q004

What is the safest way to brake?

Mark one answer

- ❍ a Brake hard, put your gear lever into neutral and pull your handbrake on just before stopping
- ❍ b Brake lightly, push your clutch pedal down and pull your handbrake on just before stopping
- ❍ c Put your gear lever into neutral, brake hard, then ease off just before stopping
- ❍ d Brake lightly, then harder as you begin to stop, then ease off just before stopping

Q005

You are driving at night and are dazzled by the headlights of an oncoming car. You should

Mark one answer

- ❍ a slow down or stop
- ❍ b close your eyes
- ❍ c flash your headlights
- ❍ d pull down the sun visor

Q006

In which situation should you expect other vehicles to overtake you on either side?

Mark one answer

- ❍ a In a one-way street
- ❍ b On a dual carriageway
- ❍ c On a motorway
- ❍ d In a contraflow system

Q007

You are reversing into a side road. While reversing you should look mainly

Mark one answer

- ❍ a into the interior mirror
- ❍ b into the door mirror nearest the kerb
- ❍ c into the door mirror away from the kerb
- ❍ d through the rear window

Q008

When turning your car in the road, you should

Mark one answer

- ❍ a use a driveway if possible
- ❍ b overhang the kerb
- ❍ c check all around for other road users
- ❍ d keep your hand on the handbrake throughout

Q009

You should ONLY use a hand-held telephone

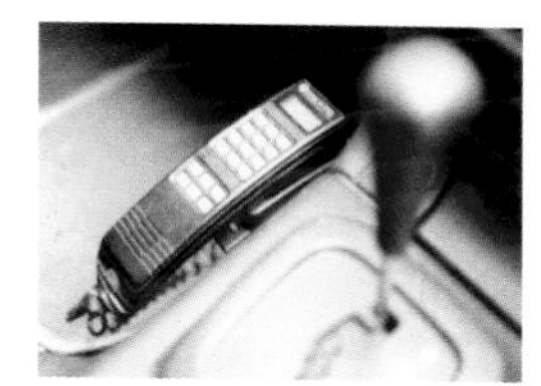

Mark one answer

- ❍ a if your vehicle has an automatic gear change
- ❍ b if you need to make an emergency call
- ❍ c when you have stopped at a safe place
- ❍ d when travelling on a minor road

Q010

To move off safely from a parked position, you should

Mark one answer

- ❍ a use your mirrors and look round for a final check
- ❍ b signal if other drivers need to slow down
- ❍ c NOT look round if there is a parked vehicle close in front of you
- ❍ d give a hand signal as well as using your indicator

Q011

You wish to overtake a long, slow-moving vehicle on a busy road. You should

Mark one answer

- ❍ a keep well back until you can see that it is clear
- ❍ b wait behind until the driver waves you past
- ❍ c flash your headlights for the oncoming traffic to give way
- ❍ d follow it closely and keep moving out to see the road ahead

Answers and Explanations

Q001 **c**
Q002 **b** You must not use a hand-held telephone while you are driving
Q003 **b** You should not signal until you can see it is safe to move off.
Q004 **d** Braking lightly at first and then harder reduces the risk of skidding. Easing off the brakes just before you stop avoids stopping with a jolt.
Q005 **a**
Q006 **a** But always be aware of others around you.
Q007 **d** Although you should keep looking all around, you should look mainly in the direction you are moving, which is backwards. You have most vision through the rear window.
Q008 **c**
Q009 **c**
Q010 **a**
Q011 **a**

Driving Theory Test Questions

Attitudes to Other Road Users

Q012

A vehicle has a flashing green light.
What does this mean?

Mark one answer

- ❍ a The vehicle is slow moving
- ❍ b A doctor is answering an emergency call
- ❍ c It is a motorway police patrol vehicle
- ❍ d A vehicle is carrying hazardous chemicals

Q013

You are driving towards a zebra crossing.
Pedestrians are waiting to cross.
You should

Mark one answer

- ❍ a slow down and prepare to stop
- ❍ b give way to the elderly and infirm only
- ❍ c use your headlamps to indicate they can cross
- ❍ d wave at them to cross the road

Q014

You are driving a slow-moving vehicle on a narrow winding road.
You should

Mark one answer

- ❍ a keep well out to stop vehicles overtaking dangerously
- ❍ b pull in safely when you can to let following vehicles overtake
- ❍ c wave following vehicles past you if you think they can overtake quickly
- ❍ d give a left signal when it is safe for vehicles to overtake you

Q015

You are following a vehicle on a wet road.
You should leave a time gap of at least

Mark one answer

- ❍ a 4 seconds
- ❍ b 1 second
- ❍ c 2 seconds
- ❍ d 3 seconds

Q016

You are driving a slow-moving vehicle.
There is a queue of traffic behind.
You should

Mark one answer

- ❍ a take no action
- ❍ b keep as far to the left as possible
- ❍ c wave the traffic past when the road is clear
- ❍ d pull in when it is safe to do so

Q017

You are travelling on a fast road in good conditions. How can you be sure you are following at a safe distance?

Mark one answer

- ❍ a The distance between you and the car in front should be twice the length of your vehicle
- ❍ b The distance between you and the car in front should be your braking distance
- ❍ c There should be a two-second time gap between you and the car in front
- ❍ d There should be a one-second time gap between you and the car in front

Q018

The driver behind seems to be in a hurry and is very close behind you.
You should

Mark one answer

- ❍ a signal left and wave the driver past
- ❍ b slow down and allow the driver to overtake
- ❍ c take no action and keep to the speed limit
- ❍ d move out nearer to the middle of the road

Q019

A bus is stopped at a bus stop ahead of you. Its right-hand indicator is flashing.
You should

Mark one answer

- ❍ a flash your headlights and slow down
- ❍ b sound your horn and keep going
- ❍ c slow down and then sound your horn
- ❍ d slow down and give way if it is safe to do so

Q020

You are driving a slow-moving vehicle on a narrow road. When the traffic wishes to overtake you should

Mark one answer

- ❍ a take no action
- ❍ b put your hazard-warning lights on
- ❍ c stop immediately and wave them on
- ❍ d pull in safely as soon as you can

Q021

A flashing amber light on a vehicle means

Mark one answer

- ❍ a a slow-moving vehicle
- ❍ b an emergency vehicle travelling fast
- ❍ c a doctor going to an emergency
- ❍ d a security van carrying cash

Q022

You are driving in traffic at the speed limit for the road. The driver behind is trying to overtake. You should

Mark one answer

- ❍ a move closer to the car ahead, so the driver behind has no room to overtake
- ❍ b wave the driver behind to overtake when it is safe
- ❍ c accelerate to get away from the driver behind
- ❍ d keep a steady course and allow the driver behind to overtake

Q023

A vehicle pulls out in front of you at a junction. What should you do?

Mark one answer

- ❍ a Swerve past it and blow your horn
- ❍ b Slow down and be ready to stop
- ❍ c Flash your headlights and drive up close behind
- ❍ d Accelerate past it immediately

Q024

You should ONLY flash your head lamps to other road users

Mark one answer

- ❍ a to let them know you are there
- ❍ b to show you are giving way
- ❍ c to show you are about to reverse
- ❍ d to tell them you have right of way

Q025

You are driving at the legal speed limit. A vehicle comes up quickly behind, flashing its headlamps. You should

Mark one answer

- ❍ a accelerate to maintain a gap behind you
- ❍ b touch the brakes to show your brake lights
- ❍ c allow the vehicle to overtake
- ❍ d maintain your speed and prevent the vehicle from overtaking

Q026

You are approaching a pelican crossing. The amber light is flashing. You must

Mark one answer

- ❍ a encourage pedestrians to cross
- ❍ b give way to pedestrians who are crossing
- ❍ c not move until the green light appears
- ❍ d stop even if the crossing is clear

Q027

At a pelican crossing the flashing amber light means you should

Mark one answer

- ❍ a stop, if you can do so safely
- ❍ b stop and wait for the green light
- ❍ c give way to pedestrians waiting to cross
- ❍ d give way to pedestrians already on the crossing

Q028

You are in a one-way street and want to turn right. You should position yourself

Mark one answer

- ❍ a in the left-hand lane
- ❍ b in the right-hand lane
- ❍ c in either lane, depending on the traffic
- ❍ d just left of the centre line

Q029

A two-second gap between yourself and the car in front is sufficient when conditions are

Mark one answer

- a good
- b wet
- c damp
- d foggy

Q030

You must take extra care when driving near trams because

Mark one answer

- a of their speed and silent approach
- b they may stop suddenly to re-charge the batteries
- c they are automatic and have no driver
- d you must NOT drive over the rails

Q031

What should you use your horn for?

Mark one answer

- a To allow you right of way
- b To greet other road users
- c To alert others to your presence
- d To signal your annoyance

Q032

What type of emergency vehicle is fitted with a green flashing light?

Mark one answer

- a Fire engine
- b Road gritter
- c Doctor's car
- d Ambulance

Q033

You are driving at the legal speed limit. A vehicle behind wants to overtake. Should you try to prevent the driver overtaking?

Mark one answer

- a No, unless it is safe to do so
- b Yes, because the other driver is acting dangerously
- c Yes, because the other driver is breaking the law
- d No, not at any time

Q034

Which TWO of the following are causes of rear-end collisions?

Mark two answers

- a Driving too close to the vehicle in front
- b Traffic lights changing suddenly
- c Pedestrians crossing in busy built-up areas
- d Not paying enough attention to the road
- e Stopping at every junction

Q035

You stop for pedestrians waiting to cross at a zebra crossing. They do not start to cross. What should you do?

Mark one answer

- a Sound your horn
- b Be patient and wait
- c Drive on
- d Wave them to cross

Answers and Explanations

Q012 **b** Doctors on emergency call may display a flashing green light. Slow-moving vehicles have amber flashing lights. Police, fire and ambulance service vehicles have blue flashing lights.

Q013 **a** The word 'only' makes 'b' wrong and you should never flash or wave at pedestrians to cross.

Q014 **b** 'c' is dangerous and 'd' is confusing. Other drivers might think you are stopping or turning left.

Q015 **a** In good conditions you should allow two seconds but on a wet road you double this to four.

Q016 **d** This will relieve congestion and allow traffic to pass safely.

Q017 **c** A two-second time gap is recommended by the *Highway Code*.

Q018 **c** Signalling and waving the driver past may cause further problems.

Q019 **d** This eases congestion but the other answers could cause confusion.

Q020 **d**

Q021 **a**

Q022 **d**

Q023 **b** This is the only safe thing to do. The other answers are the actions of an aggressive driver.

Q024 **a** You should only flash your headlights to warn other road users that you are there.

Q025 **c** This is the only safe option.

Q026 **b** You must give way to pedestrians already on the crossing but may drive on if the crossing is clear.

Q027 **d**

Q028 **b** To turn right from a one-way street you normally position yourself in the right-hand lane.

Q029 **a** In other conditions the gap must be increased.

Q030 **a**

Q031 **c**

Q032 **c**

Q033 **d** Even if other drivers are breaking the law or acting dangerously, you are likely to increase the danger if you try to prevent them overtaking.

Q034 **a & d** 'b', 'c' and 'e' are situations where the risk may increase, but the cause is 'd' or 'a'.

Q035 **b** Pedestrians are naturally nervous and cautious at crossings, so allow them time. Only drive on if you are certain they do not intend to cross.

Driving Theory Test Questions

Vehicle Defects, Safety Equipment and the Environment

Q036

Which FOUR of these MUST be in good working order for your car to be roadworthy?

Mark four answers

- ❍ a Speedometer
- ❍ b Oil warning light
- ❍ c Windscreen washers
- ❍ d Temperature gauge
- ❍ e Horn
- ❍ f Windscreen wipers

Q037

What is the most important factor in avoiding running into the car in front?

Mark one answer

- ❍ a Making sure your brakes are efficient
- ❍ b Always driving at a steady speed
- ❍ c Keeping the correct separation distance
- ❍ d Having tyres that meet the legal requirements

Q038

Your vehicle pulls to one side when braking. You should

Mark one answer

- ❍ a change the tyres around
- ❍ b pump the pedal when braking
- ❍ c use your handbrake at the same time
- ❍ d consult your garage as soon as possible

Q039

If you notice a strong smell of petrol as you drive along, you should

Mark one answer

- ❍ a not worry, as it is only exhaust fumes
- ❍ b carry on at a reduced speed
- ❍ c expect it to stop in a few miles
- ❍ d stop and investigate the problem

Q040

You must NOT sound your horn

Mark one answer

- ❍ a between 10:00pm and 6:00am in a built-up area
- ❍ b between 11:30pm and 7:00am in a built-up area
- ❍ c at any time in a built-up area
- ❍ d between 11:30pm and 6:00am on any road

Q041

It is important to wear suitable shoes when you are driving.
Why is this?

Mark one answer

- ❍ a To maintain safe control of the pedals
- ❍ b To prevent wear on the pedal rubbers
- ❍ c To enable you to make quicker gear changes
- ❍ d To enable you to walk for assistance if you break down

Q042

Which THREE does the law require you to keep in good condition?

Mark three answers

- ❍ a Headlights
- ❍ b Gears
- ❍ c Windscreen
- ❍ d Clutch
- ❍ e Seat belts

Q043

What will reduce the risk of neck injury resulting from a collision?

Mark one answer

- ❍ a An air-sprung seat
- ❍ b Anti-lock brakes
- ❍ c A collapsible steering wheel
- ❍ d A properly adjusted head restraint

Q044

A car driver MUST ensure that seat belts are worn by

Mark one answer

- ❍ a children under 14
- ❍ b all front seat passengers
- ❍ c all passengers
- ❍ d all rear seat passengers

Q045

Car passengers MUST wear a seat belt if one is available, unless they are

Mark one answer

- ❍ a under 14 years old
- ❍ b under 5 feet in height
- ❍ c sitting in the rear seat
- ❍ d exempt for medical reasons

Q046

Which TWO are badly affected if the tyres are under-inflated?

Mark two answers

- ❍ a Changing gear
- ❍ b Reversing
- ❍ c Braking
- ❍ d Steering

Q047

What does this warning light on the instrument panel mean?

Mark one answer

- ❍ a Warning triangle
- ❍ b Hazard flashers
- ❍ c Main beam
- ❍ d Handbrake on

Q048

When must you use dipped headlights during the day?

Mark one answer

- ❍ a All the time
- ❍ b Along narrow streets
- ❍ c In poor visibility
- ❍ d When parking

Q049

It is essential that tyre pressures are checked regularly. When should this be done?

Mark one answer

- ❍ a After any lengthy journey
- ❍ b After driving at high speed
- ❍ c When tyres are cold
- ❍ d When tyres are hot

Q050

In which of these containers may you carry petrol in a motor vehicle?

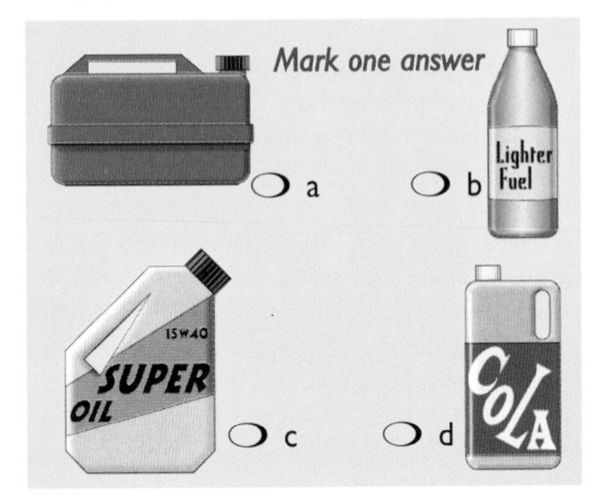

Q051

You are testing your suspension. You notice that your vehicle keeps bouncing when you press down on the front wing. What does this mean?

Mark one answer

- ❍ a Worn tyres
- ❍ b Tyres under-inflated
- ❍ c Steering wheel not located centrally
- ❍ d Worn shock absorber(s)

Q052

Why should tyres be kept to the pressure the manufacturer tells you?

Mark one answer

- ❍ a To keep the car the right height above the road
- ❍ b To save wear on the engine
- ❍ c To help prevent the car from skidding
- ❍ d To stop the car from leaning to one side

Q053

When are you allowed to drive if your brake lights do NOT work?

Mark one answer

- ❍ a During the daytime
- ❍ b At no time
- ❍ c When going for an MOT test
- ❍ d In an emergency

Q054

Which of these, if allowed to get low, could cause an accident?

Mark one answer

- ❍ a Brake fluid level
- ❍ b Anti-freeze level
- ❍ c Battery water level
- ❍ d Radiator coolant level

Q055

When may you use hazard warning lights?

Mark one answer

- ❍ a When you have broken down
- ❍ b To park alongside another car
- ❍ c To park on double yellow lines
- ❍ d When you are being towed

Q056

Excessive or uneven tyre wear can be caused by faults in which THREE?

Mark three answers

- ❍ a Wheel alignment
- ❍ b The gearbox
- ❍ c The suspension
- ❍ d The accelerator
- ❍ e The braking system
- ❍ f The exhaust system

Q057

For which TWO of these may you use hazard warning lights?

Mark two answers

- ❍ a When you are double parked on a two-way road
- ❍ b When driving on a motorway, to warn drivers behind of a hazard ahead
- ❍ c When your direction indicators are not working
- ❍ d When warning oncoming traffic that you intend to stop
- ❍ e When your vehicle has broken down and is causing an obstruction

Q058

When should you NOT use your horn in a built-up area?

Mark one answer

- ❍ a Between 8:00pm and 8:00am
- ❍ b Between 11:30 pm and 7:00am
- ❍ c Between 9:00pm and dawn
- ❍ d Between dusk and 8:00am

Q059

You are carrying two children and their parents in your car. Who is responsible for seeing that the children wear seat belts?

Mark one answer

- ❍ a The children's parents
- ❍ b You
- ❍ c The front-seat passenger
- ❍ d The children

Q060

Hazard warning lights should be used when vehicles are

Mark one answer

- ❍ a faulty and moving slowly
- ❍ b being towed along a road
- ❍ c reversing into a side road
- ❍ d broken down and causing an obstruction

Q061

Your vehicle pulls to one side when you brake. What is the most likely fault?

Mark one answer

- ❍ a Low brake fluid level
- ❍ b Your handbrake is still on
- ❍ c Poorly adjusted brakes
- ❍ d Incorrect tyre pressure

Q062

What will cause high fuel consumption?

Mark one answer

- ❍ a Poor steering control
- ❍ b Accelerating around bends
- ❍ c Harsh braking and acceleration
- ❍ d Driving in high gears

Q063

You cannot see clearly behind when reversing. What should you do?

Mark one answer

- ❍ a Ask someone to guide you
- ❍ b Open your window to look behind
- ❍ c Open the door and look behind
- ❍ d Look in the nearside mirror

Q064

It is illegal to drive with tyres that

Mark one answer

❍ a have a large, deep cut in the side wall
❍ b have been bought second-hand
❍ c are of different makes
❍ d have painted walls

Q065

The legal minimum depth of tread for car tyres over three-quarters of the breadth is

Mark one answer

❍ a 2.5 mm
❍ b 4 mm
❍ c 1.6 mm
❍ d 1 mm

Q066

What should you NEVER do at a petrol station?

Mark one answer

❍ a Run about
❍ b Eat
❍ c Smoke
❍ d Wash windscreens

Answers and Explanations

Q036 **a, c, e & f** These must, by law, be in good working order.
Q037 **c** 'c' is correct because of the words 'most important factor'. 'a' and 'd' obviously also help.
Q038 **d**
Q039 **d** Your car might catch fire if you drove on.
Q040 **b** The regulation only applies in a built-up area.
Q041 **a**
Q042 **a, c & e**
Q043 **d**
Q044 **a** If passengers are under 14 it is the driver's responsibility to ensure they wear seat belts.
Q045 **d** All passengers, front and rear. must wear seat belts, if fitted, unless exempt for medical reasons.
Q046 **c & d** Correct tyre pressures give stability and reduce the risk of skidding.
Q047 **b**
Q048 **c**
Q049 **c** Checking tyres when cold gives a more accurate reading.
Q050 **a**
Q051 **d**
Q052 **c** Incorrect tyre pressures add to the risk of skidding.
Q053 **b** It is a legal requirement to have brake lights that work.
Q054 **a** A low level of brake fluid may cause your brakes to fail.
Q055 **a** You should not use hazard warning lights when being towed, so 'd' is wrong.
Q056 **a, c & e**
Q057 **b & e**
Q058 **b**
Q059 **b** However, if someone over 14 years is in the car it is their own responsibility.
Q060 **d**
Q061 **c** Note the words 'most likely fault'. These make 'c' the correct answer.
Q062 **c** Harsh braking is one of the major causes of high fuel consumption.
Q063 **a** If you cannot see properly you need to get someone to help.
Q064 **a**
Q065 **c**
Q066 **c** This can obviously also be dangerous with vehicles in a congested area.

Driving Theory Test Questions

Weather and Road Conditions

Q067

Stopping in good conditions at 30mph takes at least

Mark one answer

❍ a 2 car lengths
❍ b 3 car lengths
❍ c 1 car length
❍ d 6 car lengths

Q068

What is the shortest overall stopping distance on a dry road from 60mph?

Mark one answer

❍ a 53 metres (175 feet)
❍ b 73 metres (240 feet)
❍ c 58 metres (190 feet)
❍ d 96 metres (315 feet)

Q069

You are braking on a wet road. Your vehicle begins to skid. What is the first thing you should do?

Mark one answer

❍ a Release the brake fully
❍ b Quickly pull up the handbrake
❍ c Push harder on the brake pedal
❍ d Put your foot on the clutch

Q070

Coasting the vehicle

Mark one answer

❍ a improves the driver's control
❍ b makes steering easier
❍ c uses more fuel
❍ d reduces the driver's control

Q071

You are on a good dry road surface and in a vehicle with good brakes and tyres. What is the shortest overall stopping distance at 40 mph?

Mark one answer

❍ a 23 metres (75 feet)
❍ b 96 metres (315 feet)
❍ c 36 metres (120 feet)
❍ d 53 metres (175 feet)

Q072

How can you avoid wheel spin when driving in freezing conditions?

Mark one answer

❍ a Stay in first gear all the time
❍ b Put on your handbrake if the wheels begin to slip
❍ c Drive in as high a gear as possible
❍ d Allow the vehicle to coast in neutral

Q073

Braking distance in ice can be

Mark one answer

❍ a twice normal distance
❍ b 5 times normal distance
❍ c 7 times normal distance
❍ d 10 times normal distance

Q074

You wish to park facing downhill. What THREE things should you do?

Mark three answers

- ❍ a Turn the steering wheel towards the kerb
- ❍ b Park close to the bumper of another car
- ❍ c Put the handbrake on
- ❍ d Park with two wheels up on the kerb
- ❍ e Put the vehicle into reverse gear

Q075

You are on a long downhill slope. What should you do to help control the speed of your vehicle?

Mark one answer

- ❍ a Grip the steering wheel tightly
- ❍ b Select a low gear
- ❍ c Select neutral
- ❍ d Put the clutch down

Q076

You are turning left on a slippery road. The back of your vehicle slides to the right. What should you do?

Mark one answer

- ❍ a Brake firmly and do not turn the steering wheel
- ❍ b Steer carefully to the right
- ❍ c Use the clutch and brake firmly
- ❍ d Turn only to the left

Q077

In very hot weather, the road surface can get soft. Which TWO of the following will be affected most?

Mark two answers

- ❍ a The suspension
- ❍ b The windscreen
- ❍ c The steering
- ❍ d Braking

Q078

When driving in fog in daylight you should use

Mark one answer

- ❍ a dipped headlights
- ❍ b side lights
- ❍ c full beam headlights
- ❍ d hazard lights

Q079

When approaching a right-hand bend you should keep well to the left. Why is this?

Mark one answer

- ❍ a To overcome the effect of the road's slope
- ❍ b It improves your view of the road
- ❍ c It lets faster traffic from behind overtake
- ❍ d To be positioned safely if the vehicle skids

Q080

When driving in icy conditions the steering becomes light because the tyres

Mark one answer

- ❍ a have less grip on the road
- ❍ b have more grip on the road
- ❍ c are too soft
- ❍ d are too hard

Q081

Your overall stopping distance will be much longer when driving

Mark one answer

- ❍ a in fog
- ❍ b at night
- ❍ c in strong winds
- ❍ d in the rain

Q082

You have driven through a flood. What is the first thing you should do?

Mark one answer

- ❍ a Test your brakes
- ❍ b Stop and check the tyres
- ❍ c Stop and dry the brakes
- ❍ d Switch on your windscreen wipers

Q083

You are at a junction with limited visibility. You should

Mark one answer

- ❍ a inch forward, looking both ways
- ❍ b inch forward, looking to the right
- ❍ c inch forward, looking to the left
- ❍ d be ready to move off quickly

Q084

You are about to go down a steep hill. To control the speed of your vehicle you should

Mark one answer

- ❍ a select a low gear and use the brakes carefully
- ❍ b select a high gear and use the brakes carefully
- ❍ c select a high gear and use the brakes firmly
- ❍ d select a low gear and avoid using the brakes

Q085

You are driving in freezing conditions. Which THREE should you do when approaching a sharp bend?

Mark three answers

- ❍ a Accelerate into the bend
- ❍ b Avoid sudden steering movements
- ❍ c Gently apply your handbrake
- ❍ d Slow down before you reach the bend
- ❍ e Drive in as high a gear as you can
- ❍ f Keep your clutch down throughout

Q086

Freezing conditions affect the distance it takes you to come to a stop. You should expect stopping distances to increase by up to

Mark one answer

- ❍ a 2 times
- ❍ b 5 times
- ❍ c 3 times
- ❍ d 10 times

Q087

You are driving on an icy road. How can you avoid wheel spin?

Mark one answer

- ❍ a Use the handbrake if the wheels start to slip
- ❍ b Drive at a slow speed in as high a gear as possible
- ❍ c Brake gently and repeatedly
- ❍ d Drive in a low gear at all times

Q088

You are driving in a built-up area. You approach a speed hump. You should

Mark one answer

- ❍ a move across to the left-hand side of the road
- ❍ b slow your vehicle right down
- ❍ c wait for any pedestrians to cross
- ❍ d stop and check both pavements

Q089

You are driving in heavy rain when your steering suddenly becomes very light. To get control again you must

Mark one answer

- ❍ a change down to a lower gear
- ❍ b brake lightly to reduce speed
- ❍ c steer towards a dry part of the road
- ❍ d ease off the accelerator

Q090

You are on a fast open road in good conditions. For safety, the distance between you and the vehicle in front should be

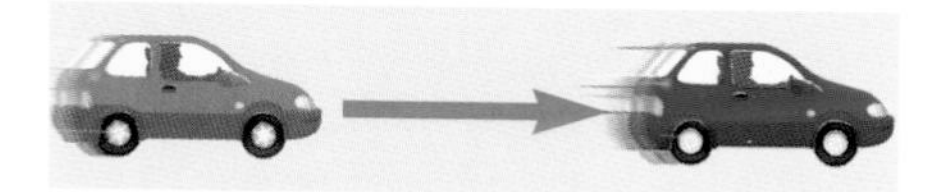

Mark one answer

- ❍ a a two-second time gap
- ❍ b one car length
- ❍ c two metres (seven feet)
- ❍ d two car lengths

Q091

You are driving at 50mph in good conditions. What would be your shortest stopping distance?

Mark one answer

- ❍ a 23 metres (75 feet)
- ❍ b 53 metres (175 feet)
- ❍ c 36 metres (120 feet)
- ❍ d 73 metres (240 feet)

Q092

You are travelling at 50mph on a good dry road. What is your overall stopping distance?

Mark one answer

- ❍ a 36 metres (120 feet)
- ❍ b 75 metres (245 feet)
- ❍ c 53 metres (175 feet)
- ❍ d 96 metres (315 feet)

Q093

When driving in snow it is best to keep in as high a gear as possible. Why is this?

Mark one answer

❍ a To help you slow down quickly when you brake
❍ b So that wheel spin does not cause your engine to run too fast
❍ c To help prevent wheel spin
❍ d To leave a lower gear available in case of wheel spin

Q094

In windy conditions you need to take extra care when

Mark one answer

❍ a using the brakes
❍ b making a hill start
❍ c turning into a narrow road
❍ d passing pedal cyclists

Q095

You are coming up to a right-hand bend. You should

Mark one answer

❍ a keep well to the left as it makes the bend faster
❍ b keep well to the left for a better view around the bend
❍ c keep well to the right to avoid anything in the gutter
❍ d keep well to the right to make the bend less sharp

Q096

Where are you most likely to be affected by a crosswind?

Mark one answer

❍ a On a narrow country lane
❍ b On an open stretch of road
❍ c On a busy stretch of road
❍ d On a long, straight road

Q097

What is the braking distance at 50mph?

Mark one answer

❍ a 38 metres (125 ft)
❍ b 55 metres (180 ft)
❍ c 24 metres (79 ft)
❍ d 14 metres (46 ft)

Q098

How can you tell when you are driving over black ice?

Mark one answer

❍ a Your steering would feel light
❍ b It would be easier to brake
❍ c The noise from your tyres would sound louder
❍ d You would see black ice on the road

Q099

What is the shortest stopping distance at 70mph?

Mark one answer

❍ a 53 metres (175 feet)
❍ b 60 metres (200 feet)
❍ c 96 metres (315 feet)
❍ d 73 metres (240 feet)

Q100

What is the main reason why your stopping distance is longer after heavy rain?

Mark one answer

- a You may not be able to see large puddles
- b The brakes will be cold because they are wet
- c Your tyres will have less grip on the road
- d Water on the windscreen will blur your view of the road ahead

Q101

You are travelling behind another vehicle at 55mph. What distance would you stay behind for safety?

Mark one answer

- a 55 metres (180 feet)
- b 25 metres (80 feet)
- c 45 metres (150 feet)
- d 35 metres (115 feet)

Q102

You are driving in good conditions at 55mph. What is a safe minimum distance between you and the vehicle in front?

Mark one answer

- a 55 metres (180 feet)
- b 35 metres (115 feet)
- c 65 metres (215 feet)
- d 75 metres (245 feet)

Answers and Explanations

Q067 d The diagram on the back cover of the *Highway Code* illustrates this.

Q068 b

Q069 a Note that the question asks for the first thing you should do, which is always to remove the cause of the skid – in this case braking. You would next need to re-apply the brakes more gently. 'c' is wrong because braking harder would increase the skid.

Q070 d Coasting means driving along with the clutch pedal down. This disconnects the engine and gears from the drive wheels of the car, so you have less control.

Q071 c

Q072 c

Q073 d Braking distances can be twice normal in the wet but 10 times normal on ice.

Q074 a, c & e The handbrake and selecting reverse gear should stop the car rolling forwards. Turning the wheels towards the kerb is an added precaution. If the car rolled forward it would probably stop when the front wheels touched the kerb.

Q075 b You should ideally have selected the lower gear before starting down the slope. Both 'c' and 'd' would be likely to make your car go faster as you would no longer be in any gear at all.

Q076 b To correct a rear wheel skid you turn the wheel in the

direction you are skidding – in this case to the right.

Q077 c & d

Q078 a Sidelights are not enough so 'b' is wrong. Full beam headlights tend to reflect back the fog, so 'c' is also incorrect.

Q079 b You can see further round the bend earlier if you keep to the left.

Q080 a

Q081 d

Q082 a Your brakes may be wet. So the first thing you should do is check them and then dry them out if necessary.

Q083 a You cannot go until you can see that it is safe, so you need to inch forward until you can see clearly in both directions.

Q084 a A low gear will help control your speed, but on a steep hill you will also need your brakes.

Q085 b, d & e

Q086 d

Q087 b Wheel spin is caused by too much acceleration. The less grip the tyres have on the road, the more wheel spin is likely, and on icy roads the tyres have very little grip. A slow speed is essential and a high gear keeps the wheels turning more gently for the speed.

Q088 b

Q089 d This problem is sometimes called aquaplaning. Your tyres build up a thin film of water between them and the road and lose all grip. The steering suddenly feels light and probably uncontrollable. The solution is to ease off the accelerator until you feel the tyres grip the road again.

Q090 a This is the 'two-second rule'.

Q091 b

Q092 c

Q093 c

Q094 d In windy conditions cyclists are all too easily blown about and caused to wobble or steer off course.

Q095 b

Q096 b You can be affected by crosswinds anywhere, but the 'most likely' place is on an open stretch of road.

Q097 a Note this is the braking distance. The overall stopping distance is further because you have to add 'thinking' distance.

Q098 a Black ice is normally invisible when you are driving. The tyres will lose grip with the road which will make the steering feel light.

Q099 c

Q100 c

Q101 a

Q102 a

Impairment

Q103

You are not sure if your cough medicine will affect your driving. What TWO things could you do?

Mark two answers

- ❍ a Ask your doctor
- ❍ b Check the medicine label
- ❍ c Drive if you feel alright
- ❍ d Ask a friend or relative for advice

Q104

You are taking drugs which are likely to affect your driving. What should you do?

Mark one answer

- ❍ a Seek medical advice before driving
- ❍ b Limit your driving to essential journeys
- ❍ c Only drive if accompanied by a full licence holder
- ❍ d Drive only for short distances

Q105

Your doctor has given you a course of medicine. Why should you ask if it is OK to drive?

Mark one answer

- ❍ a Some types of medicine can cause your reactions to slow down
- ❍ b Drugs make you a better driver by quickening your reactions
- ❍ c You will have to let your insurance company know about the medicine
- ❍ d The medicine you take may affect your eyesight

Q106

Which THREE of these are likely effects of drinking alcohol on driving?

Mark three answers

- ❍ a Reduced co-ordination
- ❍ b Increased confidence
- ❍ c Poor judgement
- ❍ d Increased concentration
- ❍ e Faster reactions
- ❍ f Colour blindness

Q107

What are THREE ways that drinking alcohol can affect driving?

Mark three answers

- ❍ a It slows down your reactions
- ❍ b It reduces your confidence
- ❍ c It reduces your co-ordination
- ❍ d It affects your judgement of speed

Q108

When driving what is the maximum legal level for alcohol in your blood?

Mark one answer

- ❍ a 50 mg per 100 ml
- ❍ b 60 mg per 100 ml
- ❍ c 80 mg per 100 ml
- ❍ d 90 mg per 100 ml

Q109

You should NOT drive if

Mark one answer

- ❍ a you suffer from cramps
- ❍ b you suffer from hay fever
- ❍ c you feel tired or unwell
- ❍ d you have just passed your test

Q110

If you are feeling tired it is best to stop as soon as you can. Until then you should

Mark one answer

- ❍ a ensure a supply of fresh air
- ❍ b increase your speed to find a stopping place quickly
- ❍ c gently tap the steering wheel
- ❍ d keep changing speed to improve concentration

Q111

What advice should you give to a driver who has had a few alcoholic drinks at a party?

Mark one answer

- ❍ a Go home by public transport
- ❍ b Have a strong cup of coffee and then drive home
- ❍ c Drive home carefully and slowly
- ❍ d Wait a short while and then drive home

Q112

Another driver does something that upsets you. You should

Mark one answer

- ❍ a let them know how you feel
- ❍ b flash your headlamps several times
- ❍ c try not to react
- ❍ d sound your horn

Q113

You are planning to drive a long distance. Which THREE things will make the journey safer?

Mark three answers

- ❍ a Avoid travelling at night
- ❍ b Avoid motorways
- ❍ c Ensure a supply of fresh air
- ❍ d Make stops for refreshments
- ❍ e Drive slowly

Q114

Which THREE are likely to make you lose concentration while driving?

Mark three answers

- ❍ a Using your windscreen washers
- ❍ b Looking in your wing mirror
- ❍ c Listening to loud music
- ❍ d Looking at road maps
- ❍ e Using a mobile phone

Q115

You are about to drive home. You cannot find the glasses you need to wear when driving. You should

Mark one answer

- ❍ a drive home slowly, keeping to quiet roads
- ❍ b find a way of getting home without driving
- ❍ c borrow a friend's glasses and drive home
- ❍ d drive home at night, so that the lights will help you

Q116

You are about to drive but you feel ill. You should

Mark one answer

- ❍ a take suitable medicine before driving
- ❍ b shorten the journey if you can
- ❍ c not drive
- ❍ d promise yourself an early night

Q117

How does alcohol affect your driving?

Mark one answer

- ❍ a It speeds up your reactions
- ❍ b It increases your awareness
- ❍ c It improves your co-ordination
- ❍ d It reduces your concentration

Q118

A driver can only read a number plate at the required distance with glasses on. The glasses should be worn

Mark one answer

- ❍ a only when driving long distances
- ❍ b all the time when driving
- ❍ c only when reversing
- ❍ d only in poor visibility

Q119

How often should you stop on a long journey?

Mark one answer

- ❍ a When you need petrol
- ❍ b At least every four hours
- ❍ c At least every two hours
- ❍ d When you need to eat

Q120

If you start to feel tired on your journey you should

Mark one answer

- ❍ a stop and eat a large meal
- ❍ b stop immediately and take deep breaths
- ❍ c complete the journey then have a good sleep
- ❍ d stop and have a short nap or some strong coffee

Q121

A driver attends a social event. What precautions should the driver take?

Mark one answer

- ❍ a Drink plenty of coffee after drinking alcohol
- ❍ b Avoid busy roads after drinking alcohol
- ❍ c Avoid drinking alcohol on an empty stomach
- ❍ d Avoid drinking alcohol completely

Q122

You are driving on a motorway. You feel tired. You should

Mark one answer

- ❍ a carry on but drive slowly
- ❍ b leave the motorway at the next exit
- ❍ c stop on the hard shoulder
- ❍ d complete your journey as quickly as possible

Q123

A driver pulls out of a side road in front of you. You have to brake hard. You should

Mark one answer

- ❍ a flash your lights to show your annoyance
- ❍ b ignore the error and stay calm
- ❍ c sound your horn to show your annoyance
- ❍ d overtake as soon as possible

Q124

Which THREE result from drinking alcohol and driving?

Mark three answers

- ❍ a False sense of confidence
- ❍ b Faster reactions
- ❍ c Greater awareness of danger
- ❍ d Less control
- ❍ e Poor judgement of speed

Q125

You take some cough medicine given to you by a friend. What must you do before driving?

Mark one answer

- ❍ a Check the label to see if the medicine will affect your driving
- ❍ b Drink some strong coffee
- ❍ c Ask your friend if taking the medicine affected their driving
- ❍ d Make a short journey to see if the medicine is affecting your driving

Q126

You find that you need glasses to read vehicle number plates. When must you wear them?

Mark one answer

- ❍ a Only in bad weather conditions
- ❍ b Only when you think it necessary
- ❍ c Only in bad light or at night time
- ❍ d At all times when driving

Q127

To drive you must be able to read a number plate from what distance?

Mark one answer

- ❍ a 10 metres (22 feet)
- ❍ b 20.5 metres (67 feet)
- ❍ c 205 metres (673 feet)
- ❍ d 15 metres (49 feet)

Q128

Which TWO things would help keep you alert during a long journey?

Mark two answers

- ❍ a Finish your journey as fast as you can
- ❍ b Keep off the motorways and use country roads
- ❍ c Make regular stops for refreshments
- ❍ d Make sure you get plenty of fresh air

Q129

Which one of the following is NOT affected by alcohol?

Mark one answer

- ❍ a Perception of colours
- ❍ b Judgement of speed
- ❍ c Reaction time
- ❍ d Co-ordination

Answers and Explanations

Q103 **a & b**

Q104 **a** A significant number of drugs, even those that you can buy in the chemist, can affect your ability to drive. Sometimes a warning is given on the packet, but if in any doubt seek medical advice.

Q105 **a** The answer required is 'a', but do remember that 'd' is also possible, particularly if the medicine was related to an eye problem.

Q106 **a, b & c** 'd' and 'e' are a problem because this tends to be how you think after drinking and not how you actually are.

Q107 **a, c & d** Drinking tends to falsely increase your confidence which makes 'b' wrong.

Q108 **c** 35 microgrammes per 100 ml of breath, 80 milligrammes per 100 ml of blood, 107 milligrammes per 100 ml of urine. As you go down the body the figure goes up, is an easy way to help remember.

Q109 **c**

Q110 **a**

Q111 **a** The only sensible answer is don't drink and drive.

Q112 **c** However hard, the safest course is to try not to react and since the increase in 'road rage' this is even more essential. Reacting tends to increase danger or raise the risk of violence.

Q113 **a, c & d** Fresh air and refreshment help keep you alert and you are more likely to be most able to concentrate during the daylight hours. Motorways are statistically our safest roads so 'f' is wrong.

Q114 **c, d & e** 'a' and 'b' are normal parts of the driving task.

Q115 **b** It is illegal to drive if you cannot satisfy the requirements of the eyesight test.

Q116 **c**

Q117 **d** You may well feel, after drinking, that 'a', 'b', and 'c' are true, which is never correct but makes you dangerous.

Q118 **b**

Q119 **c**

Q120 **d**

Q121 **d** The golden rule – if you intend to drive DO NOT DRINK ALCOHOL.

Q122 **b** If you feel tired you greatly increase your chances of having an accident. You must stop, but as you are on a motorway you cannot do this unless you leave at the next exit or find a service station before it.

Q123 **b** 'a', 'c' and 'd' can only make matters worse. So 'b' is correct. You should certainly stay calm and ignore the error in the sense of not reacting to it. You should not ignore it to the extent of taking no notice. Next time you may predict such an error before it happens and be able to stay safe without braking hard.

Q124 **a, d, & e**

Q125 **a**

Q126 **d** If you need glasses to drive you must wear them whenever you are driving, so 'd' is correct.

Q127 **b** Glasses or contact lenses may be worn.

Q128 **c & d**

Q129 **a**

Driving Theory Test Questions

Hazard Perception

Q130

What THREE things should the driver of the grey car be specially aware of?

Mark three answers

- a The bumpy road surface
- b Pedestrians stepping out between cars
- c Cars leaving parking spaces
- d Empty parking spaces
- e Other cars behind the grey car
- f Parked cars' doors opening

Q131

What should the driver of the red car do?

Mark one answer

- a Wave the pedestrians who are waiting to cross
- b Quickly drive behind the pedestrian in the road
- c Wait for the pedestrian in the road to cross
- d Tell the pedestrian in the road she should not have crossed

Q132

What is the main hazard shown in this picture?

Mark one answer

- a The cyclist crossing the road
- b Vehicles turning right
- c Vehicles doing U-turns
- d Parked cars around the corner

Q133

What should the driver of the grey car (arrowed) do?

Mark one answer

- a Reverse out of the box junction
- b Wait in the same place until the lights are green
- c Wait until the lights are red then cross
- d Cross if the way is clear

Q134

What should the driver of the red car (arrowed) do?

Mark one answer

- ❍ a Sound the horn to tell other drivers where he is
- ❍ b Squeeze through the gap
- ❍ c Wave the driver of the white car to go on
- ❍ d Wait until the car blocking the way has moved

Q135

What should the cars on the pelican crossing have done?

Mark one answer

- ❍ a Left a space in the queue of traffic
- ❍ b Got closer to the cars in front
- ❍ c Put their hazard warning lights on
- ❍ d Waited before the zigzag lines

Q136

What should the driver of the white car do?

Mark one answer

- ❍ a Stop and let the pedestrian cross
- ❍ b Wave the pedestrian to go back
- ❍ c Drive on slowly
- ❍ d Stop only if there is a car behind

Q137

Which road user has caused a hazard?

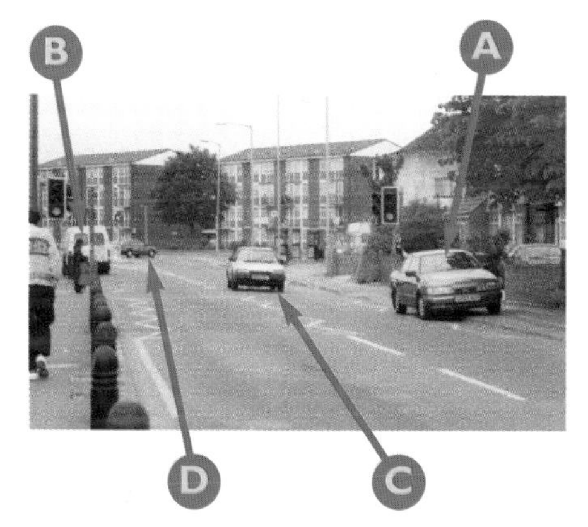

Mark one answer

- ❍ a The parked car (A)
- ❍ b The pedestrian waiting to cross (B)
- ❍ c The moving car (C)
- ❍ d The car turning (D)

Q138

The driver of which car has caused a hazard?

Mark one answer

- ❍ a Car A
- ❍ b Car B
- ❍ c Car C
- ❍ d Car D

Q139

What should the driver of a car coming up to this level crossing do?

Mark one answer

- ❍ a Drive through quickly
- ❍ b Stop before the barrier
- ❍ c Drive through carefully
- ❍ d Switch on hazard warning lights

Q140

What are TWO main hazards a driver should be aware of when driving along this street?

Mark two answers

- ❍ a Glare from the sun
- ❍ b Lack of road markings
- ❍ c Car doors opening suddenly
- ❍ d The headlights of parked cars being switched on
- ❍ e Children running out from between vehicles
- ❍ f Large goods vehicles

Q141

What should the driver of the car approaching the crossing do?

Mark one answer

- ❍ a Continue at the same speed
- ❍ b Sound the horn
- ❍ c Drive through quickly
- ❍ d Slow and get ready to stop

Q142

What is the main hazard the driver of the red car (arrowed) should be most aware of?

Mark one answer

- ❍ a The bus may move out into the road
- ❍ b Glare from the sun may affect the driver's vision
- ❍ c The black car may stop suddenly
- ❍ d Oncoming vehicles will assume the driver is turning right

Q143

What is the main hazard a driver should be aware of when following this cyclist?

Mark one answer

- ❍ a The cyclist may move into the left and dismount
- ❍ b The cyclist may swerve out into the road
- ❍ c The contents of the cyclist's carrier may fall onto the road
- ❍ d The cyclist may wish to turn right at the end of the road

Q144

In heavy motorway traffic you are being followed closely by the vehicle behind. How can you lower the risk of an accident?

Mark one answer

- ❍ a Tap your foot on the brake pedal
- ❍ b Switch on your hazard lights
- ❍ c Move on to the hard shoulder and stop
- ❍ d Increase your distance from the vehicle in front

Answers and Explanations

Q130	**b, c & f**
Q131	**c**
Q132	**a**
Q133	**d**
Q134	**d**
Q135	**a**
Q136	**c**
Q137	**a**
Q138	**a**
Q139	**b**
Q140	**c & e**
Q141	**d**
Q142	**a**
Q143	**b**
Q144	**d**

Driving Theory Test Questions

Other Road Users

Q145

Which TWO should you allow extra room when overtaking?

Mark two answers

- ❍ a Tractors
- ❍ b Motorcycles
- ❍ c Road sweeping vehicles
- ❍ d Bicycles

Q146

The approach to a zebra crossing is marked with zigzag lines. Which TWO must you NOT do within the marked area?

Mark two answers

- ❍ a Cross the lines
- ❍ b Drive at more than 10mph
- ❍ c Overtake
- ❍ d Park

Q147

What lane will horse riders take when going round a roundabout?

Mark one answer

- ❍ a Right
- ❍ b Left
- ❍ c Centre
- ❍ d Between centre and right

Q148

Look at this picture. What is the danger you should be most aware of?

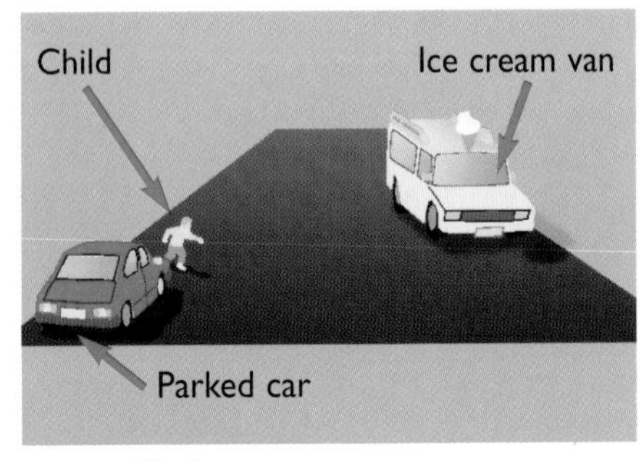

Mark one answer

- ❍ a The child may run into the road
- ❍ b The ice cream van may move off
- ❍ c The driver of the ice cream van may get out
- ❍ d The car on the left may move off

Q149

You are turning left into a side road. Pedestrians are crossing the road near the junction. You must

Mark one answer

- ❍ a wait for them to cross
- ❍ b wave them on
- ❍ c sound your horn
- ❍ d switch on your hazard lights

Q150

Where in particular should you look out for motorcyclists?

Mark one answer

- ❍ a In a filling station
- ❍ b At a road junction
- ❍ c Near a service area
- ❍ d When entering a car park

Q151

You are about to reverse into a side road. A pedestrian wishes to cross behind you. You should

Mark one answer

- ❍ a wave to the pedestrian to stop
- ❍ b wave to the pedestrian to cross
- ❍ c give way to the pedestrian
- ❍ d reverse before the pedestrian starts to cross

Q152

You are approaching a school crossing patrol. When this sign is held up you must

Mark one answer

- ❍ a stop and beckon the children to cross
- ❍ b stop and allow any children to cross
- ❍ c stop only if the children are on a pedestrian crossing
- ❍ d stop only when the children are actually crossing the road

Q153

You are waiting to come out of a side road. Why should you watch carefully for motorcycles?

Mark one answer

- ❍ a Motorcycles are usually faster than cars
- ❍ b Police patrols often use motorcycles
- ❍ c Motorcycles are small and hard to see
- ❍ d Motorcycles have right of way

Q154

You see some horse riders as you approach a roundabout. They are signalling right but keeping well to the left. You should

Mark one answer

- ❍ a proceed as normal
- ❍ b keep close to them
- ❍ c cut in front of them
- ❍ d stay well back

Q155

Which age group is most likely to be involved in a road accident?

Mark one answer

- ❍ a 17 to 25 year-olds
- ❍ b 36 to 45 year-olds
- ❍ c 46 to 55 year-olds
- ❍ d 55 year-olds and over

Q156

You are driving in town. There is a bus at the bus stop on the other side of the road. Why should you be careful?

Mark one answer

- ❍ a The bus may have broken down
- ❍ b The bus may move off suddenly
- ❍ c Pedestrians may come from behind the bus
- ❍ d The bus may remain stationary

Q157

You are turning left from a main road into a side road. People are already crossing the road into which you are turning. You should

Mark one answer

- ❍ a wait and allow them to cross
- ❍ b continue, as it is your right of way
- ❍ c signal to them to continue crossing
- ❍ d sound your horn to warn them of your presence

Q158

What is the most common factor in causing road accidents?

Mark one answer

- ❍ a Driver error
- ❍ b Weather conditions
- ❍ c Road conditions
- ❍ d Mechanical failure

Q159

You are driving behind a cyclist. You wish to turn left just ahead. You should

Mark one answer

- ❍ a overtake the cyclist before the junction
- ❍ b pull alongside the cyclist and stay level until after the junction
- ❍ c go around the cyclist on the junction
- ❍ d hold back until the cyclist has passed the junction

Q160

A horse rider is in the left lane approaching a roundabout. The driver behind should expect the rider to

Mark one answer

- ❍ a turn right
- ❍ b go in any direction
- ❍ c turn left
- ❍ d go ahead

Q161

You want to turn right from a junction but your view is restricted by parked vehicles. What should you do?

Mark one answer

- ❍ a Move out quickly but be prepared to stop
- ❍ b Sound your horn and pull out if there is no reply
- ❍ c Stop, get out and look along the main road to check
- ❍ d Stop, then move slowly forward until you have a clear view

Q162

You have just passed your driving test. How likely are you to have an accident compared with other drivers?

Mark one answer

❍ a More likely
❍ b It depends on your age
❍ c Less likely
❍ d About the same

Q163

You see a pedestrian carrying a white stick. This shows that the person is

Mark one answer

❍ a disabled
❍ b blind
❍ c elderly
❍ d deaf

Q164

You are driving past a line of parked cars. You notice a ball bouncing out into the road ahead. What should you do?

Mark one answer

❍ a Continue driving at the same speed and sound your horn
❍ b Continue driving at the same speed and flash your headlights
❍ c Slow down and be prepared to stop for children
❍ d Stop and wave the children across to fetch their ball

Q165

You are reversing around a corner when you notice a pedestrian walking behind you. What should you do?

Mark one answer

❍ a Slow down and wave the pedestrian across
❍ b Continue reversing and steer round the pedestrian
❍ c Continue reversing and sound your horn
❍ d Stop and give way

Q166

Where should you take particular care to look out for motorcyclists and cyclists?

Mark one answer

❍ a On dual carriageways
❍ b At zebra crossings
❍ c At junctions
❍ d On one way streets

Q167

Which sign means there may be people walking along the road?

Mark one answer

❍ a ❍ b

❍ c ❍ d

Q168

You are approaching the roundabout and see the cyclist signal right. Why is the cyclist keeping to the left?

Mark one answer

❍ a It is a quicker route for the cyclist
❍ b The cyclist is slower and more vulnerable
❍ c The cyclist is going to turn left instead
❍ d The cyclist thinks the *Highway Code* does not apply to bicycles

Q169

You notice horse riders in front. What should you do FIRST?

Mark one answer

❍ a Pull out to the middle of the road
❍ b Accelerate around them
❍ c Signal right
❍ d Be prepared to slow down

Q170

You see someone step onto the road holding this sign. What must you do?

Mark one answer

❍ a Slow down and look out for children
❍ b Signal the person to cross
❍ c Pull up before the person
❍ d Drive carefully round the person

Q171

How should you overtake horse riders?

Mark one answer

❍ a Drive slowly and leave plenty of room
❍ b Drive up close and overtake as soon as possible
❍ c Speed is not important but allow plenty of room
❍ d Use your horn just once to warn them

Q172

You see a pedestrian with a white stick and two red reflective bands. This means the person is

Mark one answer

❍ a physically disabled
❍ b deaf and dumb
❍ c deaf and blind
❍ d blind and dumb

Q173

You are at a road junction turning into a minor road. There are pedestrians crossing the minor road. You should

Mark one answer

- ❍ a stop and wave the pedestrians across
- ❍ b sound your horn to let the pedestrians know you are there
- ❍ c carry on, the pedestrians should give way to you
- ❍ d give way to the pedestrians who are already crossing

Q174

You are coming up to a roundabout. A cyclist is signalling to turn right. What should you do?

Mark one answer?

- ❍ a Give the cyclist plenty of room
- ❍ b Overtake on the right
- ❍ c Give a horn warning
- ❍ d Signal the cyclist to move across

Q175

Your vehicle hits a pedestrian at 40mph. The pedestrian

Mark one answer

- ❍ a will certainly be killed
- ❍ b will probably be killed
- ❍ c will certainly survive
- ❍ d will probably survive

Q176

You are overtaking a motorcyclist. What should you do?

Mark one answer

- ❍ a Try to pass on a bend
- ❍ b Move over to the opposite side of the road
- ❍ c Pass close by and as quickly as possible
- ❍ d Give as much room as you would for a car

Q177

How will a school crossing patrol signal you to stop?

Mark one answer

- ❍ a By pointing to children on the opposite pavement
- ❍ b By displaying a stop sign
- ❍ c By displaying a red light
- ❍ d By giving you an arm signal

Q178

You are following a car driven by an elderly driver. You should

Mark one answer

- ❍ a expect the driver to drive badly
- ❍ b be aware that the driver's reactions may not be as fast as yours
- ❍ c flash your lights and overtake
- ❍ d stay close behind and drive carefully

Q179

When you park your vehicle you must NOT

Mark one answer

- ❍ a park on a major road
- ❍ b obstruct other road users
- ❍ c leave it in gear
- ❍ d leave the sidelights on

Q180

When passing animals you should NOT

Mark one answer

- ❍ a rev the engine or sound the horn
- ❍ b change down to a lower gear
- ❍ c use your direction indicators
- ❍ d have any lights on

Q181

Which THREE should you do when passing sheep on a road?

Mark three answers

- ❍ a Allow plenty of room
- ❍ b Pass quickly but quietly
- ❍ c Drive very slowly
- ❍ d Briefly sound your horn
- ❍ e Be ready to stop

Q182

You are driving on a country road. What should you expect to see coming towards you on YOUR side of the road?

Mark one answer

- ❍ a Pedestrians
- ❍ b Motorcycles
- ❍ c Bicycles
- ❍ d Horse riders

Q183

A school crossing patrol shows a stop children sign. What must you do?

Mark one answer

- ❍ a Continue if safe to do so
- ❍ b Slow down and be ready to stop
- ❍ c Stop at all times
- ❍ d Stop ONLY if children are crossing

Q184

In which THREE places would parking your vehicle cause danger or obstruction to other road users?

Mark three answers

- ❍ a On your driveway
- ❍ b In front of a property entrance
- ❍ c At or near a bus stop
- ❍ d On the approach to a level crossing
- ❍ e In a marked parking space

Q185

You are driving on a narrow country road. Where would you find it most difficult to see horses and riders ahead of you?

Mark one answer

- ❍ a When travelling downhill
- ❍ b When travelling uphill
- ❍ c On right-hand bends
- ❍ d On left-hand bends

Q186

You are turning left at a junction. Pedestrians have started to cross the road. You should

Mark one answer

- ❍ a go on giving them plenty of room
- ❍ b stop and wave at them to cross
- ❍ c give way to them
- ❍ d blow your horn and proceed

Q187

You should NEVER attempt to overtake a cyclist

Mark one answer

- ❍ a just before you turn left
- ❍ b just before you turn right
- ❍ c on a one-way street
- ❍ d on a dual carriageway

Q188

As a new driver, how can you decrease your risk of accidents on the motorway?

Mark one answer

- ❍ a By taking further training
- ❍ b By keeping up with the car in front
- ❍ c By never driving over 45mph
- ❍ d By driving only in the nearside lane

Q189

When may you stop on a pedestrian crossing?

Mark one answer

- ❍ a Not at any time
- ❍ b Where there is a queue of traffic in front of you
- ❍ c Between the hours of 11:00 pm and 7:00 am
- ❍ d To avoid an accident

Q190

When you are overtaking a cyclist, you should leave as much room as you would give to a car. Why is this?

Mark one answer

- ❍ a The cyclist might change lanes
- ❍ b The cyclist might get off the bike
- ❍ c The cyclist might have to make a right turn
- ❍ d The cyclist might swerve

Q191

As you are driving along you meet a group of horses and riders from a riding school. Why should you be extra cautious?

Mark one answer

- ❍ a They will be moving in single file
- ❍ b They will be moving slowly
- ❍ c Many of the riders may be learners
- ❍ d The horses will panic more because they are in a group

Q192

You are driving behind two cyclists. They approach a roundabout in the left-hand lane. In which direction should you expect the cyclists to go?

Mark one answer

- ❍ a Left
- ❍ b Right
- ❍ c Any direction
- ❍ d Straight ahead

Q193

Why should you allow extra room when overtaking a motorcyclist on a windy day?

Mark one answer

- ❍ a The rider may turn off suddenly to get out of the wind
- ❍ b The rider may stop suddenly
- ❍ c The rider may be blown across in front of you
- ❍ d The rider may be travelling faster than normal

Q194

What does this sign warn you to look for?

Mark one answer

- ❍ a Schoolchildren
- ❍ b A school-crossing patrol
- ❍ c A pedestrian crossing
- ❍ d A park

Answers and Explanations

Q145 **b & d** Motorcycles and bicycles can easily wobble off course and you need to allow them extra room.

Q146 **c & d** You must never park on the zigzag lines. To be exact, you must not overtake the moving motor vehicle nearest the crossing or the leading vehicle which has stopped to give way to a pedestrian.

Q147 **b** 'b' is the answer required, but always stay back and give horse riders room.

Q148 **a** All are potential dangers but the child is the greatest risk.

Q149 **a** When you turn into a side road pedestrians who are already crossing have priority so you must give way.

Q150 **b** Note the words 'in particular' in the question which makes 'b' correct. Most accidents happen at or near road junctions.

Q151 **c**

Q152 **b** You must always stop at any stop sign and you should never beckon or wave anyone to cross.

Q153 **c**

Q154 **d** Animals can easily be frightened, so always give them plenty of room.

Q155 **a**

Q156 **c**

Q157 **a**

Q158 **a** Statistics show that about 95 per cent of accidents involve an element of human error.

Q159 **d** As the question states you are turning left JUST ahead, you have no time to overtake the cyclist safely which is why 'a' is incorrect.

Q160 **b**

Q161 **d** You cannot turn right until you can see it is safe to do so. You should stop and then edge slowly forwards until you can see clearly to the left and right.

Q162 **a** Your chances of having an accident are greatest in the first two years after passing your test regardless of your age.

Q163 **b**

Q164 **c**

Q165 **d**

Q166 **c**

Q167 **a** Red triangles give warnings, in this case of people walking along the road. 'c' is a warning of a pedestrian crossing.

Q168 **b** We can, of course, only guess why the cyclist is acting in this way, but 'b' is the most likely reason and the answer required.

Q169 **d** Horses and their riders can be unpredictable so 'd' is the safest first action.

Q170 **c** You must stop at a stop sign, in this case held by a school-crossing patrol.

Q171 **a**

Q172 **c**

Q173 **d**

Q174 **a**

Q175 **b** When pedestrians are about 'Kill your speed'.

Q176 **d** Like cyclists, motor cyclists may wobble when affected by crosswinds.

Q177 **b**

Q178 **b**

Q179 **b**

Q180 **a**

Q181 **a, c & e**

Q182 **a** Pedestrians are the most likely to expect as country roads often have no pavements and pedestrians are advised to walk on the right so that they can see oncoming traffic on their side of the road. However, you should always expect the unexpected when driving.

Q183 **c** You must stop at a stop sign, so 'c' is correct. However, don't forget that if you spot the sign early enough you may be able to slow down sufficiently that by the time you reach the school patrol the sign has been removed and the crossing is clear.

Q184 **b, c & d**

Q185 **d** While 'd' is correct, remember that narrow country roads often have banks, hedges, trees or other obstructions to your view as well as bends, so sometimes 'c' might also be true.

Q186 **c**

Q187 **a** The word 'NEVER' makes 'a' correct.

Q188 **a** The other three possible answers are all potentially dangerous and 'a' is correct.

Q189 **d** You should never stop where you would block a pedestrian crossing except to prevent an accident.

Q190 **d** 'd' is the answer required but you should also be aware that cyclists can be unpredictable.

Q191 **c** The word 'extra' points to 'c' as the correct answer. In all situations you should be cautious when passing horses.

Q192 **c** Cyclists tend to keep to the left and you must always expect the unexpected.

Q193 **c**

Q194 **a**

Driving Theory Test Questions

Other Vehicle Characteristics

Q195

Which of these vehicles is LEAST likely to be affected by crosswinds?

Mark one answer

❍ a Cyclists
❍ b Motorcyclists
❍ c Cars
❍ d High-sided vehicles

Q196

Before overtaking a large vehicle you should keep well back. Why is this?

Mark one answer

❍ a To get the best view of the road ahead
❍ b To give acceleration space to overtake quickly on blind bends
❍ c To leave a gap in case the vehicle stops and rolls back
❍ d To offer other drivers a safe gap if they want to overtake you

Q197

You are following a long vehicle approaching a crossroads. The driver signals right but moves close to the left-hand kerb. What should you do?

Mark one answer

❍ a Warn the driver of wrong signal
❍ b Wait behind the long vehicle
❍ c Report the driver to the police
❍ d Overtake on the right-hand side

Q198

Why is passing a lorry more risky than passing a car?

Mark one answer

❍ a Lorries may suddenly pull up
❍ b Lorries are longer than cars
❍ c The brakes of lorries are not as good
❍ d Lorries climb hills more slowly

Q199

You are following a large articulated vehicle. It is going to turn left into a narrow road. What action should you take?

Mark one answer

❍ a Move out and overtake on the offside
❍ b Pass on the left as the vehicle moves
❍ c Overtake quickly before the lorry moves out
❍ d Be prepared to stop behind

Q200

In which THREE places could a strong crosswind affect your course?

Mark three answers

- a In tunnels
- b After overtaking a large vehicle
- c In towns
- d When passing gaps in hedges
- e When passing parked vehicles
- f On exposed sections of roadway

Q201

You are approaching a mini-roundabout. The long vehicle in front is signalling left but positioned over to the right. You should

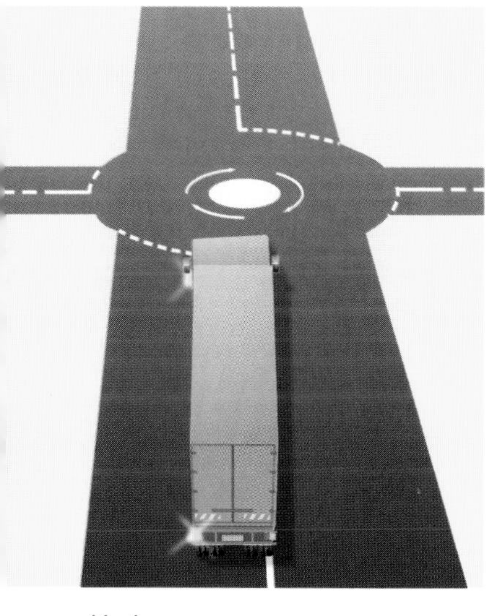

Mark one answer

- a sound your horn
- b overtake on the left
- c follow the same course as the lorry
- d keep well back

Q202

You are following a long vehicle. It approaches a crossroads and signals left but moves out to the right. You should

Mark one answer

- a get closer in order to pass it quickly
- b assume the signal is wrong and it is really turning left
- c stay well back and give it room
- d overtake as it starts to slow down

Q203

It is very windy. You are behind a motorcyclist who is overtaking a high-sided vehicle. What should you do?

Mark one answer

- a Overtake the motorcyclist immediately
- b Keep well back
- c Stay level with the motorcyclist
- d Keep close to the motorcyclist

Q204

You are driving on a wet motorway with surface spray. You should

Mark one answer

- a use dipped headlights
- b use your hazard flashers
- c use your rear fog lights
- d drive in any lane with no traffic

Q205

When about to overtake a long vehicle you should

Mark one answer

- ❍ a sound the horn to warn the driver you are there
- ❍ b stay well back from the lorry to obtain a better view
- ❍ c drive close to the lorry in order to pass more quickly
- ❍ d flash your lights and wait for the driver to signal to you when it is safe

Q206

When you approach a bus signalling to move off from a bus stop, you should

Mark one answer

- ❍ a get past before it moves
- ❍ b allow it to pull away if safe
- ❍ c flash your headlamps as you approach
- ❍ d signal left and wave the bus on

Q207

The FIRST thing you should do when you want to overtake a large lorry is

Mark one answer

- ❍ a stay well back to get a better view
- ❍ b move close behind so you can pass quickly
- ❍ c keep in close to the left-hand side
- ❍ d flash your headlights and wait for the driver to wave you on

Q208

You are following a large lorry on a wet road. Spray makes it difficult to see. You should

Mark one answer

- ❍ a put your headlights on full beam
- ❍ b keep close to the lorry, away from the spray
- ❍ c drop back until you can see better
- ❍ d speed up and overtake quickly

Q209

Motorcyclists are more vulnerable than car drivers because they

Mark one answer

- ❍ a ride at higher speeds
- ❍ b take corners at higher speeds
- ❍ c are affected more by changes in road surface
- ❍ d can accelerate faster than cars

Q210

The road is wet. Why might a motorcyclist steer round drain covers on a bend?

Mark one answer

- ❍ a To avoid puncturing the tyres on the edge of the drain covers
- ❍ b To help judge the bend using the drain covers as marker points
- ❍ c To prevent the motorcycle sliding on the metal drain covers
- ❍ d To avoid splashing pedestrians on the pavement

Q211

You wish to overtake a long, slow-moving vehicle on a busy road. You should

Mark one answer

- ❍ a wait behind until the driver waves you past
- ❍ b keep well back until you can see it is clear
- ❍ c flash your headlights for the oncoming traffic to give way
- ❍ d follow it closely and keep moving out to see the road ahead

Answers and Explanations

Q195 c Of the four mentioned, cars are by far the most stable and least affected by crosswinds.

Q196 a You cannot see ahead if you are too close to a large vehicle in front of you.

Q197 b Long vehicles require more space to turn and often need to position to account for this.

Q198 b Overtaking takes time, so the longer the vehicle you overtake the greater the danger as you will take longer to pass it.

Q199 d The large articulated vehicle may need to position to the right in order to turn left into the narrow road.

Q200 b, d & f Strong crosswinds could affect you almost anywhere, but 'b', 'd' and 'f' are the most likely places and the correct answers.

Q201 d

Q202 c

Q203 b Let the motorcyclist complete the overtake before even thinking about following.

Q204 a Spray reduces visibility. You should use dipped headlights when visibility is reduced.

Q205 b This increases your field of vision.

Q206 b This helps traffic flow without giving confusing signals.

Q207 a This allows you the visibility and space to plan the overtaking manoeuvre.

Q208 c

Q209 c Two-wheeled vehicles can easily be thrown off course.

Q210 c Water on metal is a dangerous combination, especially for a two-wheeled vehicle.

Q211 b

Driving Theory Test Questions

Own Vehicle Handling

Q212

You are driving on a well-lit motorway at night. You must

Mark one answer

❍ a use only your sidelights
❍ b always use rear fog lights
❍ c always use your headlights
❍ d use headlights only in bad weather

Q213

Which TWO of the following are correct? When overtaking at night you should

Mark two answers

❍ a be careful because you can see less
❍ b wait until a bend so you can see the oncoming headlights
❍ c sound your horn twice before moving out
❍ d put your headlights on full beam
❍ e beware of bends in the road ahead

Q214

Which TWO are correct? The passing places on a single track road are

Mark two answers

❍ a to turn the car around in, if you are lost
❍ b to pull into if an oncoming vehicle wants to proceed
❍ c for taking a rest from driving
❍ d for stopping and checking your route
❍ e to pull into if the car behind wants to overtake

Q215

You are overtaking a car at night. You must be sure that

Mark one answer

❍ a you do not dazzle other road users
❍ b you flash your headlamps before overtaking
❍ c your rear fog lights are switched on
❍ d you have switched your lights to full beam before overtaking

Q216

In which THREE of these situations may you overtake another vehicle on the left?

Mark three answers

❍ a When you are in a one-way street
❍ b When approaching a motorway slip road where you will be turning off
❍ c When the vehicle in front is signalling to turn right
❍ d When a slower vehicle is travelling in the right-hand lane of a dual-carriageway
❍ e In slow-moving traffic queues when traffic in the right-hand lane is moving more slowly

Q217

You should only use rear fog lights when you cannot see further than about

Mark one answer

❍ a 100 metres (108 yds)
❍ b 200 metres (215 yds)
❍ c 250 metres (270 yds)
❍ d 150 metres (162 yds)

Q218

Why is 'coasting' wrong?

Mark one answer

- a It will cause the car to skid
- b It will make the engine stall
- c There is no engine braking
- d The engine will run faster

Q219

You are driving on a motorway in fog. The left-hand edge of the motorway can be identified by the reflective studs. What colour are they?

Mark one answer

- a Green
- b Amber
- c Red
- d White

Q220

Travelling at night, you are dazzled by headlights coming towards you. You should

Mark one answer

- a pull down your sun visor
- b switch on your main beam headlights
- c put your hand over your eyes
- d slow down or stop

Q221

You should switch your rear fog lights on when visibility drops below

Mark one answer

- a your overall stopping distance
- b 10 car lengths
- c 10 metres
- d 100 metres

Q222

What are TWO main reasons why 'coasting' downhill is wrong?

Mark two answers

- a You have less braking and steering control
- b The vehicle will pick up speed
- c Petrol consumption will be higher
- d It puts more wear and tear on the tyres
- e It damages the engine

Q223

You are following other vehicles in fog, with your lights on. How else can you reduce the chances of being involved in an accident?

Mark one answer

- a Use your main beam instead of dipped headlights
- b Reduce your speed and increase the gap
- c Keep close to the vehicle in front
- d Keep together with the faster vehicles

Q224

You are on a narrow road at night.
A slower-moving vehicle ahead has been signalling right for some time.
What should you do?

Mark one answer

- ❍ a Overtake on the left
- ❍ b Wait for the signal to be cancelled before overtaking
- ❍ c Flash your headlights before overtaking
- ❍ d Signal right and sound your horn

Q225

To correct a rear wheel skid you should

Mark one answer

- ❍ a not turn at all
- ❍ b turn away from it
- ❍ c turn into it
- ❍ d apply your handbrake

Q226

Why should you test your brakes after this hazard?

Mark one answer

- ❍ a Because you will be driving on a slippery road
- ❍ b Because your brakes would be soaking wet
- ❍ c Because you would have driven down a long hill
- ❍ d Because you would have just crossed a long bridge

Q227

You should not drive with your foot on the clutch for longer than necessary because

Mark one answer

- ❍ a it reduces your control of the vehicle
- ❍ b it increases the wear on the gearbox
- ❍ c it increase petrol consumption
- ❍ d it reduces the grip of the tyres

Q228

You wish to overtake on a dual carriageway. You see in your mirror that the car behind has pulled out to overtake you. You should

Mark one answer

- ❍ a signal and pull out to overtake
- ❍ b signal to tell the driver behind that you also want to overtake
- ❍ c touch the brakes to show your brake lights
- ❍ d not signal until the car has passed

Q229

You have to park on the road in fog.
You should

Mark one answer

- ❍ a leave dipped headlights and fog lights on
- ❍ b leave dipped headlights on
- ❍ c leave sidelights on
- ❍ d leave main beam headlights on

Q230

You are following a vehicle at a safe distance on a wet road. Another driver overtakes you and pulls into the gap you had left. What should you do?

Mark one answer

- ❍ a Flash your headlights as a warning
- ❍ b Try to overtake safely as soon as you can
- ❍ c Drop back to regain a safe distance
- ❍ d Stay close to the other vehicle until it moves on

Q231

How can you best control your vehicle when driving in snow?

Mark one answer

- ❍ a By staying in low gear and gripping the steering wheel tightly
- ❍ b By driving in first gear
- ❍ c By keeping the engine revs high and slipping the clutch
- ❍ d By driving slowly in as high a gear as possible

Q232

You are driving in the left-hand lane of a dual carriageway. Another vehicle overtakes and pulls in front of you leaving you without enough separation distance. You should

Mark one answer

- ❍ a drop back
- ❍ b move to the right lane
- ❍ c continue as you are
- ❍ d sound your horn

Q233

You have to make a journey in foggy conditions. You should

Mark one answer

- ❍ a leave plenty of time for your journey
- ❍ b follow closely other vehicles' tail lights
- ❍ c never use de-misters and windscreen wipers
- ❍ d keep two seconds behind other vehicles

Q234

You are driving on a motorway at night. You MUST have your headlights switched on unless

Mark one answer

- ❍ a your vehicle is broken down on the hard shoulder
- ❍ b there are vehicles close in front of you
- ❍ c you are travelling below 50mph
- ❍ d the motorway is lit

Q235

You are driving along a major road with many side roads. What precautions should you take?

Mark one answer

- ❍ a Sound your horn as your reach each side road
- ❍ b Slow down in case a vehicle pulls out
- ❍ c Stop at each side road and check for traffic
- ❍ d Keep well out near the centre of the road

Q236

You see a vehicle coming towards you on a single-track road. You should

Mark one answer

❍ a reverse back to the main road
❍ b stop at a passing place
❍ c do an emergency stop
❍ d put on your hazard flashers

Q237

How should you drive around a bend on ice?

Mark one answer

❍ a Using the clutch and brake together
❍ b Slowly and smoothly
❍ c In first gear
❍ d Braking as you enter the bend

Q238

You are driving in fog. The car behind seems to be very close. You should

Mark one answer

❍ a switch on your hazard warning lights
❍ b pull over and stop immediately
❍ c speed up to get away
❍ d continue cautiously

Q239

You are dazzled by oncoming headlights when driving at night. What should you do?

Mark one answer

❍ a Brake hard
❍ b Drive faster past the oncoming car
❍ c Flash your lights
❍ d Slow down or stop

Q240

You are travelling on a motorway at night with other vehicles just ahead of you. Which lights should you have on?

Mark one answer

❍ a Front fog lights
❍ b Main beam headlights
❍ c Dipped headlights
❍ d Side lights only

Q241

You are driving in poor visibility weather. You can see more than 100m ahead. How can you make sure other drivers can see you?

Mark one answer

❍ a Follow the vehicle in front closely
❍ b Turn on your rear fog lights
❍ c Turn on your dipped headlights
❍ d Keep well out towards the middle of the road

Q242

You intend to park on a road at night without lights. Which of the following is right?

Mark one answer

❍ a Your vehicle must be visible from at least 10 metres (32 feet)
❍ b You must park facing opposite the traffic flow
❍ c You must park at least half of your vehicle on the pavement
❍ d The road must have a speed limit of 30mph or less

Q243

Which THREE of the following will affect your stopping distance?

Mark three answers

- a How fast you are going
- b The time of day
- c The street lighting
- d The tyres on your vehicle
- e The weather

Q244

Why should you always reduce your speed when driving in fog?

Mark one answer

- a Because the brakes do not work as well
- b Because you could be dazzled by other people's fog lights
- c Because it is more difficult to see events ahead
- d Because the engine is colder

Q245

You are driving in fog. Why should you keep well back from the vehicle in front?

Mark one answer

- a In case it changes direction suddenly
- b In case it stops suddenly
- c In case its fog lights dazzle you
- d In case its brake lights dazzle you

Q246

You have to make a journey in fog. What are the TWO most important things you should do before you set out?

Mark two answers

- a Check your lights are working
- b Make sure the windows are clean
- c Top up the radiator with anti-freeze
- d Make sure you have a warning triangle in the vehicle
- e Check the battery

Answers and Explanations

Q212 **c**

Q213 **a & e** 'a' and 'e' are the correct answers. 'b' and 'c' are dangerous, but be aware that as you overtake 'd' may be necessary, particularly if the vehicle you overtake dips its headlights as you overtake it.

Q214 **b & e**

Q215 **a** You may need to switch to full-beam headlights as you overtake, but not before.

Q216 **a, c & e**

Q217 **a**

Q218 **c** You are coasting when you push down the clutch, disconnecting both engine and gearbox.

Q219 **c** Red reflective studs separate the left-hand lane and the hard shoulder.

Q220 **d**

Q221 **d** Remember to switch them off when the visibility improves.

Q222 **a & b**

Q223 **b**

Q224 **b**

Q225 c This answer refers to steering. For example, if the back of your car skids to the right you should turn the wheel carefully to the right to correct it.

Q226 b After driving through water your brakes will be wet, and wet brakes are inefficient.

Q227 a Driving with the clutch down ('coasting') reduces control.

Q228 d If you signal as described in 'b' you may confuse the driver behind who may assume you intend to pull out immediately, so 'd' is safest.

Q229 c

Q230 c This may feel irritating, particularly if the circumstance is repeated several times. However, it is safest and, in reality, causes you no delay.

Q231 d This gives a greater safety margin and avoids wheel spin.

Q232 a You need to adjust your separation distance continually. Don't get annoyed by this – it keeps you safe and does not add to your journey time.

Q233 a The *Highway Code* advises you to allow more time for your journey in foggy conditions. However, always ask yourself if the journey really is necessary.

Q234 a You must use your headlights on motorways at night even if the motorway is lit.

Q235 b Even though you have priority, junctions spell danger. You need to drive at a speed that will allow you to stop if another driver makes a mistake, does not see you or misjudges your speed and pulls out in front of you.

Q236 b Bear in mind that single-track roads may have passing places at long intervals. You may meet an oncoming vehicle at a point where one of you will need to reverse to the previous nearest passing point.

Q237 b The more gentle your movements on ice, the less likely you are to skid. You need as high a gear as possible, gentle use of the accelerator, a low speed and as little use of the brakes as possible.

Q238 d

Q239 d

Q240 c Full-beam headlights would dazzle the drivers in front by reflecting in their mirrors.

Q241 c This is the safest way to be seen. 'a' is obviously dangerous. 'b' is illegal as visibility is more than 100 metres and anyway only helps drivers behind. 'd' could cause an accident if an oncoming driver has the same idea.

Q242 d

Q243 a, d & e

Q244 c Everybody knows this but an alarming number of people don't put the knowledge into practice. Accidents happen as a result.

Q245 b If the car in front stops suddenly you may run into it if you have been driving too close. If it changes direction left or right it will have no effect on you.

Q246 a & b See and be seen are the two most crucial safety aspects of driving in fog.

Roads and Regulations – Motorways

Q247

You are driving a car on a motorway. Unless signs show otherwise, you must NOT exceed

Mark one answer

❍ a 50mph
❍ b 60mph
❍ c 70mph
❍ d 80mph

Q248

On a motorway, you may ONLY stop on the hard shoulder

Mark one answer

❍ a if you feel tired and need to rest
❍ b in an emergency
❍ c if you accidentally go past the exit that you wanted to take
❍ d to pick up a hitch-hiker

Q249

What should you use the hard shoulder of a motorway for?

Mark one answer

❍ a Stopping in an emergency
❍ b Overtaking
❍ c Stopping when you are tired
❍ d Joining the motorway

Q250

You are travelling on a motorway. What colour are the reflective studs on the left of the carriageway?

Mark one answer

❍ a Red
❍ b Green
❍ c White
❍ d Amber

Q251

You get a puncture on the motorway. You manage to get your vehicle on to the hard shoulder. You should

Mark one answer

❍ a use the emergency telephone and call for assistance
❍ b change the wheel yourself immediately
❍ c try to wave down another vehicle for help
❍ d only change the wheel if you have a passenger to help you

Q252

You have broken down on a motorway. Your vehicle is on the hard shoulder. Your passengers should

Mark one answer

❍ a leave the vehicle and wait on the embankment
❍ b stay in their seats with their seat belts on
❍ c leave the vehicle and walk to the nearest exit from the motorway
❍ d undo their seat belts but stay in their seats

Q253

You are driving on a three-lane motorway at 70mph. There is no traffic ahead. Which lane should you use?

Mark one answer

❍ a Any lane
❍ b Left lane
❍ c Middle lane
❍ d Right lane

Q254

When may you stop on a motorway?

Mark three answers

❍ a If you have to read a map
❍ b When you are tired and need a rest
❍ c If red lights show above the lanes
❍ d When told by the police
❍ e If a child in the car feels ill
❍ f In an emergency or a breakdown

Q255

What do these motorway signs show?

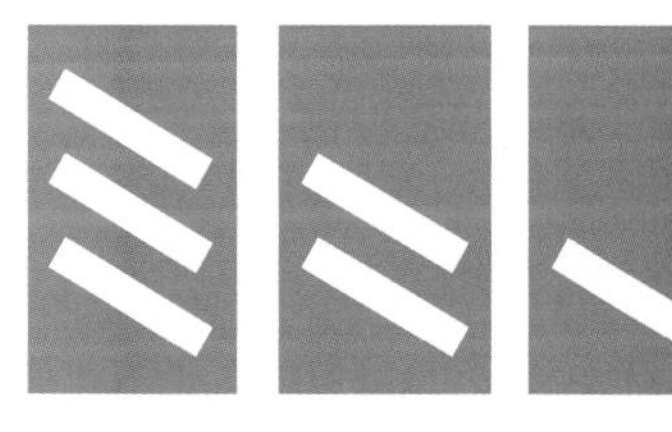

Mark one answer

❍ a They are countdown markers to a bridge
❍ b They are distance markers to the next telephone
❍ c They are countdown markers to the next exit
❍ d They warn of a police patrol ahead

Q256

Which FOUR of these must not use motorways?

Mark four answers

❍ a Learner car drivers
❍ b Horse riders
❍ c Cyclists
❍ d Motorcycles over 50cc
❍ f Double-decker buses
❍ e Farm tractors

Q257

On a three-lane motorway, which lane should you use for normal driving?

Mark one answer

❍ a Right
❍ b Centre
❍ c Left
❍ d Either the right or centre

Q258

What is the national speed limit on motorways for cars and motorcycles?

Mark one answer

❍ a 30mph
❍ b 50mph
❍ c 70mph
❍ d 60mph

Q259

You are towing a trailer on a motorway. What is your maximum speed limit?

Mark one answer

❍ a 40mph
❍ b 50mph
❍ c 70mph
❍ d 60mph

Q260

Your vehicle has broken down on a motorway. You are not able to stop on the hard shoulder. What should you do FIRST?

Mark one answer

❍ a Stop following traffic and ask for help
❍ b Attempt to repair your vehicle quickly
❍ c Switch on your hazard warning lights
❍ d Place a warning triangle in the road

Q261

You are travelling on the left-hand lane of a busy motorway. Signs indicate your lane is closed 800 yards ahead. You should

Mark one answer

❍ a signal right, then pull up and wait for someone to give way
❍ b switch on your hazard warning lights and edge over to the lane on your right
❍ c wait until you reach the obstruction, then move across to the right
❍ d move over to the lane on your right as soon as it is safe

Q262

The left-hand lane on a three-lane motorway is for use by

Mark one answer

❍ a large vehicles only
❍ b emergency vehicles only
❍ c any vehicle
❍ d slow vehicles only

Q263

Your car has broken down on the motorway. You have stopped on the hard shoulder. Where is the safest place for you to wait for help?

Mark one answer

❍ a Behind the car
❍ b In the car
❍ c In front of the car
❍ d On the grass bank

Q264

When driving through a contraflow system on a motorway you should

Mark one answer

❍ a ensure you do not exceed 30mph, for safety
❍ b switch lanes to keep the traffic flowing
❍ c drive close to the vehicle ahead to reduce queues
❍ d keep a good distance from the vehicle ahead, for safety

Q265

A basic rule when driving on motorways is

Mark one answer

❍ a use the lane that has least traffic
❍ b keep to the left lane unless overtaking
❍ c overtake on the side that is clearest
❍ d try to keep above 50mph to prevent congestion

Q266

You are joining a motorway from a slip road. You should

Mark one answer

- a match the speed of the traffic and move into a clear space
- b wait for a vehicle in the nearest lane to move over
- c wait at the beginning of the slip road for the traffic to clear
- d wait at the end of the slip road for a safe gap

Q267

You are driving on a three-lane motorway. There are red reflective studs on your left and white reflective studs to your right. Where are you?

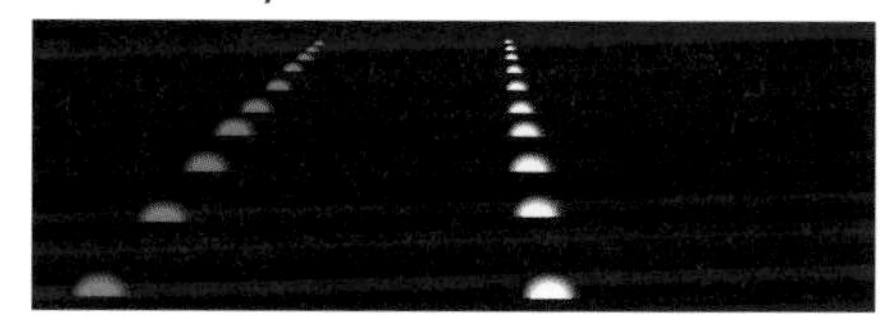

Mark one answer

- a In the right-hand lane
- b In the middle lane
- c On the hard shoulder
- d In the left-hand lane

Q268

When joining a motorway you must

Mark one answer

- a always use the hard shoulder
- b stop at the end of the acceleration lane
- c come to a stop before joining the motorway
- d always give way to traffic already on the motorways

Q269

You are driving on a motorway. There are red flashing lights above each lane. You must

Mark one answer

- a pull onto the hard shoulder
- b slow down and watch for further signals
- c leave at the next exit
- d stop and wait

Q270

The left-hand lane of a motorway should be used for

Mark one answer

- a breakdowns and emergencies only
- b overtaking slower traffic in the other lanes
- c slow vehicles only
- d normal driving

Q271

You are joining a motorway. Why is it important to make full use of the slip road?

Mark one answer

- ❍ a Because there is a space available to slow down if you need to
- ❍ b To allow you direct access to the overtaking lanes
- ❍ c To build up a speed similar to traffic on the motorway
- ❍ d Because you can continue on the hard shoulder

Q272

You are driving on a motorway. By mistake, you go past the exit which you wanted to take. You should

Mark one answer

- ❍ a carefully reverse on the hard shoulder
- ❍ b carefully reverse in the left-hand lane
- ❍ c carry on to the next exit
- ❍ d make a U-turn at the next gap in the central reservation

Q273

On a motorway the amber studs can be found between

Mark one answer

- ❍ a the hard shoulder and the carriageway
- ❍ b the central reservation and the carriageway
- ❍ c the acceleration lane and the carriageway
- ❍ d each pair of the lanes

Q274

For what reason may you use the right-hand lane of a motorway?

Mark one answer

- ❍ a For keeping out of the way of lorries
- ❍ b For overtaking other vehicles
- ❍ c For driving at more than 70mph
- ❍ d For turning right

Q275

On motorways you should never overtake on the left UNLESS

Mark one answer

- ❍ a you can see well ahead that the hard shoulder is clear
- ❍ b the traffic in the right-hand lane is signalling right
- ❍ c there is a queue of traffic to your right that is moving more slowly
- ❍ d you warn drivers behind by signalling left

Q276

What colour are the reflective studs between the lanes on a motorway?

Mark one answer

- ❍ a White
- ❍ b Green
- ❍ c Amber
- ❍ d Red

Q277

What colour are the reflective studs between a motorway and its slip road?

Mark one answer

- ❍ a Green
- ❍ b Amber
- ❍ c White
- ❍ d Red

Q278

Which of the following CAN travel on a motorway?

Mark one answer

- ❍ a Vans
- ❍ b Cyclists
- ❍ c Tractors
- ❍ d Learner drivers

Q279

Why is it particularly important to carry out a check on your vehicle before making a long motorway journey?

Mark one answer

- ❍ a High speed may increase the risk of your vehicle breaking down
- ❍ b You will have to do more harsh braking on motorways
- ❍ c Motorway service stations do not deal with breakdowns
- ❍ d The road surface will wear down the tyres faster

Q280

When are you NOT allowed to stop on the motorway?

Mark one answer

- ❍ a To prevent an accident
- ❍ b When the police tell you to
- ❍ c When there are red flashing light signals above your lane
- ❍ d To pick up something that has dropped off your vehicle

Answers and Explanations

Q247 **c**
Q248 **b**
Q249 **a** You may only stop on the hard shoulder in an emergency.
Q250 **a**
Q251 **a** Whenever you break down make sure you use your warning triangle, and keep as far from the carriageway as possible.
Q252 **a** Always leave the vehicle by the nearside door.
Q253 **b** You should always use the left-hand lane for normal driving.
Q254 **c, d & f** Do remember that motorway service areas are not officially part of the motorway.
Q255 **c** They are 100 metres (330 feet) apart.
Q256 **a, b, c & e**
Q257 **c** The other lanes should be used for overtaking.
Q258 **c** The national speed limit for cars and motorcycles is 70mph on motorways and dual carriageways and 60mph on single-lane roads.
Q259 **d** Remember that when towing a trailer strong winds can affect stability.
Q260 **c** Note that this is your FIRST action.
Q261 **d** Always look well ahead which will give plenty of time to change lanes safely.
Q262 **c** Strictly speaking, any vehicle which is allowed on a motorway.
Q263 **d** Keep children and pets under control.
Q264 **d** In these circumstances there may also be a speed limit – keep to it.
Q265 **b**
Q266 **a** Keep looking all the time and indicate your intention.
Q267 **d** Red reflective studs mark the join between the left-hand lane and the hard shoulder. White reflective studs mark the lanes.
Q268 **d**
Q269 **d**
Q270 **d**
Q271 **c** You need to build up your speed to that of the traffic already on the motorway so that you can ease into a gap in the flow of traffic.
Q272 **c** You can never reverse on a motorway.
Q273 **b**
Q274 **b**
Q275 **c**
Q276 **a**
Q277 **a**
Q278 **a**
Q279 **a** You should check oil and windscreen washer levels and also check the tyres. Plan your rest stops.
Q280 **d** Note the word 'NOT' in the question which makes 'd' the correct answer.

Driving Theory Test Questions

Roads and Regulations – Other Roads

Q281

If you see a 30mph limit ahead, this means

Mark one answer

- a the restriction applies only during the working day
- b it is a guide. You are allowed to drive 10 per cent faster
- c you must not exceed this speed
- d you must keep your speed up to 30mph

Q282

In which FOUR places must you NOT park or wait?

Mark four answers

- a At a bus stop
- b On a dual carriageway
- c Opposite a traffic island
- d In front of someone else's drive
- e On the slope of a hill
- f On the brow of a hill

Q283

Where may you overtake on a one-way street?

Mark one answer

- a Only on the left-hand side
- b Overtaking is not allowed
- c Only on the right-hand side
- d Either on the right or the left

Q284

You MUST stop when signalled to do so by which THREE of these?

Mark three answers

- a A pedestrian
- b A bus driver
- c A police officer
- d A school-crossing patrol
- e A red traffic light

Q285

What MUST you have to park in a disabled space?

Mark one answer

- a A wheelchair
- b An orange badge
- c An advanced driver certificate
- d A modified vehicle

Q286

In which TWO places must you NOT park?

Mark two answers

- a Near a police station
- b Near a school entrance
- c In a side road
- d In a one-way street
- e At a bus stop

Q287

You are driving over a level crossing. The warning lights come on and a bell rings. What should you do?

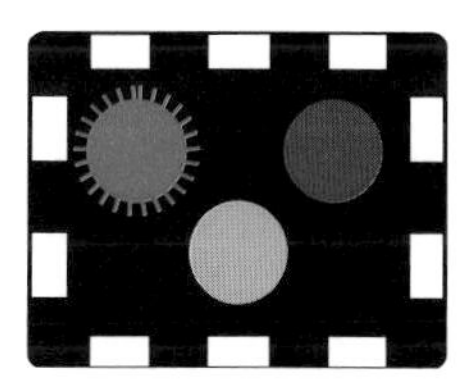

Mark one answer

- a Get everyone out of the vehicle immediately
- b Keep going and clear the crossing
- c Stop and reverse back to clear the crossing
- d Stop immediately and use your hazard warning lights

Q288

You are driving along a road which has no traffic signs. There are street lights. What is the speed limit?

Mark one answer

- a 20mph
- b 40mph
- c 30mph
- d 60mph

Q289

As a car driver, which THREE lanes must you NOT use?

Mark three answers

- a Crawler lane
- b Bus lane at the times shown
- c Cycle lane
- d Tram lane
- e Overtaking lane
- f Acceleration lane

Q290

You are going along a single-track road with passing places only on the right. The driver behind wishes to overtake. You should

Mark one answer

- a speed up to get away from the following driver
- b switch on your hazard warning lights
- c wait opposite a passing place on your right
- d drive into a passing place on your right

Q291

You are driving on a two-lane dual carriageway. For which TWO of these would you use the right-hand lane?

Mark two answers

- a Turning right
- b Overtaking slower traffic
- c Normal driving
- d Driving at the minimum allowed speed
- e Constant high speed driving
- f Mending punctures

Q292

What is the national speed limit for cars and motorcycles on a dual carriageway?

Mark one answer

- a 30mph
- b 50mph
- c 60mph
- d 70mph

Q293

At a pelican crossing, what does a flashing amber light mean?

Mark one answer

- ❍ a You must not move off until the lights stop flashing
- ❍ b You can move off, even if pedestrians are still on the crossing
- ❍ c You must stop because the lights are about to change to red
- ❍ d You must give way to pedestrians still on the crossing

Q294

You are on a road which is only wide enough for one vehicle. There is a car coming towards you. Which TWO of these would be correct?

Mark two answers

- ❍ a Pull into a passing place on your right
- ❍ b Force the other driver to reverse
- ❍ c Pull into a passing place if your vehicle is wider
- ❍ d Pull into a passing place on your left
- ❍ e Wait opposite a passing place on your left
- ❍ f Wait opposite a passing place on your right

Q295

What does a speed limit sign like this mean?

Mark one answer

- ❍ a You must not exceed the speed shown
- ❍ b It is safe to drive at the speed shown
- ❍ c The speed shown is the advised maximum
- ❍ d The speed shown allows for various road and weather conditions

Q296

You are intending to turn RIGHT at a junction. An oncoming driver is also turning right. It will normally be safer to

Mark one answer

- ❍ a keep the other vehicle to your LEFT and turn in front of it (nearside to nearside)
- ❍ b keep the other vehicle to your RIGHT and turn behind it (offside-to-offside)
- ❍ c carry on and turn at the next junction instead
- ❍ d hold back and wait for the other driver to turn first

Q297

You are driving in the right lane of a dual carriageway. You see signs showing that the right lane is closed 800 yards ahead. You should

Mark one answer

- ❍ a keep in that lane until you reach the queue
- ❍ b move to the left immediately
- ❍ c move to the left in good time
- ❍ d wait and see which lane is moving faster

Q298

You are parked in a busy high street. What is the safest way to turn your vehicle around to go the opposite way?

Mark one answer

- ❍ a Drive into a side road and reverse into the main road
- ❍ b Get someone to stop the traffic
- ❍ c Find a quiet side road to turn around in
- ❍ d Do a U-turn

Q299

When going straight ahead at a roundabout, you should

Mark one answer

- ❍ a not indicate at any time
- ❍ b indicate left before leaving the roundabout
- ❍ c indicate right when approaching the roundabout
- ❍ d indicate left when approaching the roundabout

Q300

You are leaving your vehicle parked on a road. When may you leave the engine running?

Mark one answer

- ❍ a Not on any occasion
- ❍ b If you will be parked for less than five minutes
- ❍ c If the battery is flat
- ❍ d If there is a passenger in the vehicle

Q301

When may you reverse from a side road into a main road?

Mark one answer

- ❍ a Only if both roads are clear of traffic
- ❍ b NOT at any time
- ❍ c At any time
- ❍ d Only if the main road is clear of traffic

Q302

You see this sign ahead of you. It means

Mark one answer

- ❍ a do not exceed 30mph after passing it
- ❍ b start to slow down to 30mph after passing it
- ❍ c you are leaving the 30mph speed limit area
- ❍ d the minimum speed limit ahead is 30mph

Q303

At which of these places are you sometimes allowed to park your vehicle?

Mark one answer

- ❍ a On the nearside lane of a motorway
- ❍ b On a clearway
- ❍ c On the zigzag lines of a zebra crossing
- ❍ d Where there is a single, broken yellow line

Q304

Where you see street lights but no speed limit signs, the limit is usually

Mark one answer

- ❍ a 30mph
- ❍ b 40mph
- ❍ c 50mph
- ❍ d 60mph

Q305

You are going straight ahead at a roundabout. How should you signal?

Mark one answer

- ❍ a Signal right on the approach and then left to leave the roundabout
- ❍ b Signal left as you leave the exit off the roundabout
- ❍ c Signal left as you pass the exit before the one you will take
- ❍ d Signal left on the approach to the roundabout and keep the signal on until you leave

Q306

On a three-lane dual carriageway the right-hand lane can be used for

Mark one answer

- ❍ a overtaking only, never turning right
- ❍ b fast-moving traffic only
- ❍ c turning right only, never overtaking
- ❍ d overtaking or turning right

Q307

You MUST NOT reverse

Mark one answer

- ❍ a for more than a car's length
- ❍ b into a side road
- ❍ c in a built-up area
- ❍ d for longer than necessary

Q308

You meet an obstruction on your side of the road. You must

Mark one answer

- ❍ a drive on – it is your right of way
- ❍ b wave oncoming vehicles through
- ❍ c give way to oncoming traffic
- ❍ d accelerate to get past first

Q309

Who has priority at an unmarked crossroads?

Mark one answer

- ❍ a The driver of the larger vehicle
- ❍ b The driver who is going faster
- ❍ c No one
- ❍ d The driver on the wider road

Q310

You are on a busy road and find you are travelling in the wrong direction. What should you do?

Mark one answer

- ❍ a Turn into a side road on the right and reverse into the main road
- ❍ b Turn round in a side road
- ❍ c Make a U-turn in the main road
- ❍ d Make a 'three-point' turn in the main road

Q311

On which THREE occasions MUST you stop your vehicle?

Mark three answers

- ❍ a When involved in an accident
- ❍ b At a junction with double, broken white lines
- ❍ c At a red traffic light
- ❍ d At a pelican crossing when the amber light is flashing and no pedestrians are crossing
- ❍ e When signalled to do so by a police officer

Q312

There are no speed limit signs on the road. How is a 30mph limit indicated?

Mark one answer

- ❍ a By street lighting
- ❍ b By hazard warning lines
- ❍ c By pedestrian islands
- ❍ d By double or single yellow lines

Q313

You are waiting at a level crossing. The red warning lights continue to flash after a train has passed by. What should you do?

Mark one answer

- ❍ a Continue to wait
- ❍ b Get out and investigate
- ❍ c Telephone the signal operator
- ❍ d Drive across carefully

Q314

What is the nearest you may park your vehicle to a junction?

Mark one answer

- a 10 metres (33 feet)
- b 12 metres (40 feet)
- c 15 metres (50 feet)
- d 20 metres (65 feet)

Q315

In which THREE places must you NEVER park your vehicle?

Mark three answers

- a Where there is no more pavement
- b On a 40mph road
- c Near the brow of a hill
- d Within 10 metres of a junction
- e At or near a bus stop

Q316

You are driving along a street with parked vehicles on the left-hand side. For which THREE reasons must you keep your speed down?

Mark three answers

- a Vehicles may be pulling out
- b Drivers' doors may open
- c So that oncoming traffic can see you more clearly
- d You may set off car alarms
- e Children may run out from between the vehicles

Q317

When may you enter a box junction?

Mark one answer

- a Only when there are less than two vehicles in front of you
- b Whenever the traffic lights show green
- c When your exit road is clear
- d Whenever you need to turn left

Q318

At a crossroads, there are no signs or road markings. Two vehicles approach. Which has priority?

Mark one answer

- a The vehicle travelling the fastest
- b The vehicle on the widest road
- c Vehicles approaching from the right
- d Neither vehicle

Q319

You are waiting at a level crossing. A train has passed but the lights keep flashing. You must

Mark one answer

- ❍ a phone the signal operator
- ❍ b edge over the 'STOP' line and look for trains
- ❍ c park your vehicle and investigate
- ❍ d carry on waiting

Q320

Your vehicle is parked on the road at night. When must you use side lights?

Mark one answer

- ❍ a Where you are facing oncoming traffic
- ❍ b Where the speed limit exceeds 30mph
- ❍ c Where you are near a bus stop
- ❍ d Where there are continuous white lines in the middle of the road

Answers and Explanations

Q281 **c** Red circles give orders so 'c' is correct.

Q282 **a, c, d & f**

Q283 **d** In a one-way street you are allowed to overtake on either side, provided it is safe.

Q284 **c, d & e** Note the word 'MUST' in the question, which is asking what the law says.

Q285 **b** You or your passenger may be a disabled badge-holder and entitled to park in spaces reserved for the disabled, provided you display the orange badge in your windscreen.

Q286 **b & e**

Q287 **b** You are already on the crossing when the warning lights come on, so 'b' is correct.

Q288 **c** If there are street lights, the speed limit is 30mph, unless a road sign states otherwise.

Q289 **b, c & d**

Q290 **c**

Q291 **a & b**

Q292 **d** The national speed limit is 70mph on a motorway or dual-carriageway and 60mph on two-way roads unless traffic signs denote anything different.

Q293 **d** You may drive on as soon as the crossing is clear and before the flashing amber light changes to green.

Q294 **d & f**

Q295 **a** This sign gives an order which tells you the maximum speed at which you are allowed to drive. It is a law, not a piece of advice and does not in any way imply that it

will always be safe to drive at that speed.

Q296 **b** You can see the oncoming traffic more easily from this position.

Q297 **c** 'b' is incorrect because it may not be safe to move to the left immediately.

Q298 **c** 'a' would be illegal, 'b' is silly and 'd' is dangerous because you are on a busy street.

Q299 **b** You should signal left just as you pass the exit before the one you want to take.

Q300 **a**

Q301 **b**

Q302 **a** You should adjust your speed so that you are travelling at no more than 30mph as you pass the sign.

Q303 **d** You are NEVER allowed to park at 'a', 'b' or 'c'.

Q304 **a** If there is any difference there would be repeated signs on the light posts.

Q305 **c** This is correct for most roundabouts. Bear in mind that some roundabouts do not have an exit to the left, so the first exit is straight ahead.

Q306 **d**

Q307 **d**

Q308 **c**

Q309 **c** An unmarked crossroads has no road signs or road markings and no vehicle has priority even if one road is wider or busier than the other.

Q310 **b** It is illegal to reverse from a minor to a major road so 'a' is wrong. 'c' and 'd' would be dangerous because the road is busy.

Q311 **a, c & e** 'b' is wrong because although the double, broken white lines at a junction mean 'give way', you do not necessarily have to stop in order to do so. 'd' is wrong because you may drive on at a pelican crossing when the amber light is flashing if no pedestrians are crossing.

Q312 **a**

Q313 **a** You should wait for three minutes. If no further train passes you should telephone the signal operator.

Q314 **a**

Q315 **c, d & e**

Q316 **a, b & e**

Q317 **c**

Q318 **d**

Q319 **d**

Q320 **b** You are not allowed to park at 'c' or 'd' at any time; 'a' is wrong because you must park on the left at night unless in a one-way street.

Driving Theory Test Questions

Signs and Signals

Q321

Where can you find amber studs on a motorway?

Mark one answer

- ❍ a Separating the slip road from the motorway
- ❍ b On the right-hand edge of the road
- ❍ c On the left-hand edge of the road
- ❍ d Separating the lanes

Q322

What does this traffic sign mean?

Mark one answer

- ❍ a Slippery road ahead
- ❍ b Danger ahead
- ❍ c Tyres liable to punctures ahead
- ❍ d Service area ahead

Q323

What does this sign mean?

Mark one answer

- ❍ a Do not overtake
- ❍ b Keep in one lane
- ❍ c Priority to traffic coming towards you
- ❍ d Form two lanes

Q324

You want to turn right at a junction, but you think that your indicators cannot be seen clearly. What should you do?

Mark one answer

- ❍ a Give an arm signal as well as an indicator signal
- ❍ b Get out and check if your indicators can be seen
- ❍ c Stay in the left-hand lane
- ❍ d Keep well over to the right

Q325

At this junction there is a stop sign with a solid white line on the road surface. Why?

Mark one answer

- ❍ a Speed on the major road is de-restricted
- ❍ b It is a busy junction
- ❍ c There are hazard warning lines in the centre of the road
- ❍ d Visibility along the major road is restricted

Q326

Which type of sign tells you NOT to do something?

Mark one answer

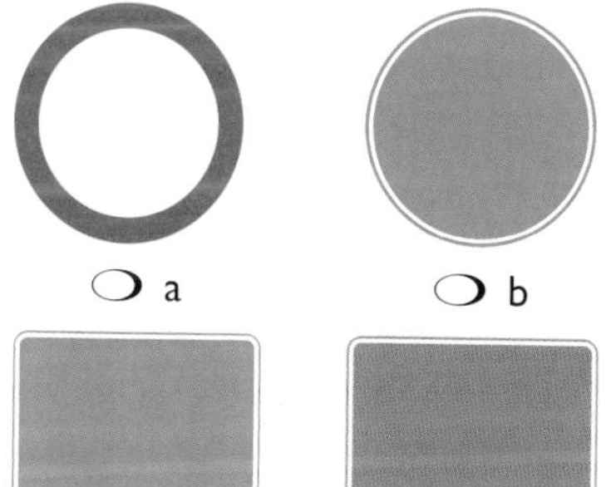

❍ a ❍ b

❍ c ❍ d

Q327

You are in the left-hand lane at traffic lights. You are waiting to turn left. At which of these traffic lights must you NOT move on?

Mark one answer

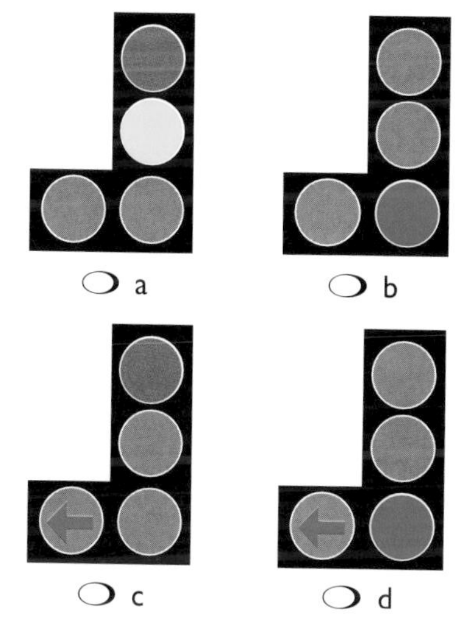

❍ a ❍ b

❍ c ❍ d

Q328

Which THREE are legally authorised to direct traffic?

Mark three answers

❍ a A traffic warden
❍ b A farm worker in charge of livestock crossing the road
❍ c A teacher in charge of children who are crossing the road
❍ d Anyone assisting the driver of a large vehicle to reverse
❍ e A roadworker operating a stop-go board
❍ f A school-crossing warden

Q329

What does this sign mean?

Mark one answer

❍ a No overtaking
❍ b You are entering a one-way street
❍ c You have priority over vehicles from the opposite direction
❍ d Two-way traffic ahead

Q330

When motorists flash their headlights at you it means

Mark one answer

❍ a there is a radar speed trap ahead
❍ b they are giving way to you
❍ c they are warning you of their presence
❍ d there is something wrong with your vehicle

Q331

What should you do when you see this sign?

Mark one answer

- ❍ a Stop ONLY if traffic is approaching
- ❍ b Stop ONLY if children are waiting to cross
- ❍ c Stop ONLY if a red light is showing
- ❍ d Stop even if the road is clear

Q332

Which sign means NO motor vehicles allowed?

Mark one answer

Q333

Where on a motorway would you find green reflective studs?

Mark one answer

- ❍ a Separating driving lanes
- ❍ b At slip road entrances and exits
- ❍ c Between the hard shoulder and the carriageway
- ❍ d Between the carriageway and the central reservation

Q334

What does this sign mean?

Mark one answer

- ❍ a No motor vehicles
- ❍ b No through road
- ❍ c End of bus lane
- ❍ d End of motorway

Q335

What does a circular traffic sign with a blue background do?

Mark one answer

- ❍ a Give warning of a motorway ahead
- ❍ b Give an instruction
- ❍ c Give directions
- ❍ d Give motorway information

Q336

What is the meaning of this traffic sign?

Mark one answer

- ❍ a You have priority over vehicles coming towards you
- ❍ b End of two-way road
- ❍ c Give priority to vehicles coming towards you
- ❍ d Bus lane ahead

Q337

Which is a HAZARD WARNING line?

Mark one answer

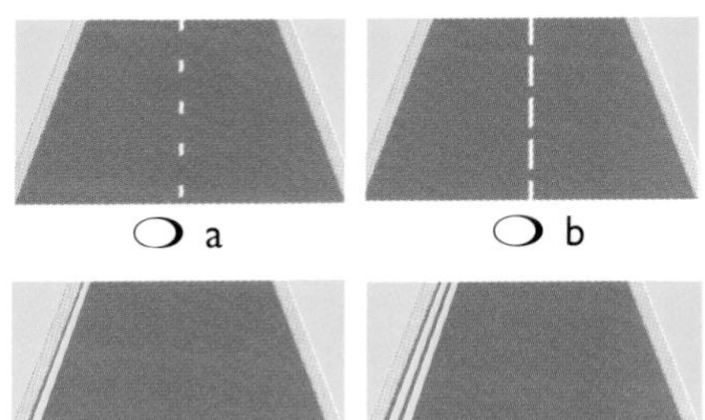

❍ a
❍ b
❍ c
❍ d

Q338

What do these zigzag lines at pedestrian crossings mean?

Mark one answer

❍ a Parking allowed only for a short time
❍ b No parking at any time
❍ c Slow down to 20mph
❍ d Sounding horns is not allowed

Q339

You are driving on a motorway. Red flashing lights appear above your lane. What should you do?

Mark one answer

❍ a Continue in that lane and await further information
❍ b Drive on to the hard shoulder
❍ c Stop and wait for an instruction to proceed
❍ d Go no further in that lane

Q340

Which sign means no vehicles are allowed?

Mark one answer

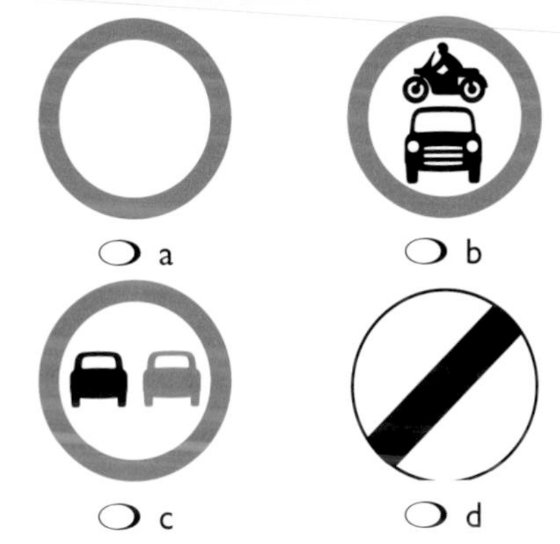

❍ a
❍ b
❍ c
❍ d

Q341

What does this sign mean?

Mark one answer

❍ a Service area 30 miles ahead
❍ b Minimum speed 30mph
❍ c Maximum speed 30mph
❍ d Lay-by 30 miles ahead

Q342

What does this sign mean?

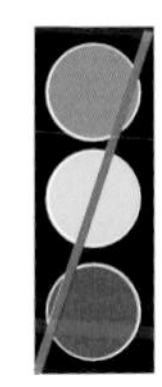

Mark one answer

❍ a Amber signal out of order
❍ b Temporary traffic lights ahead
❍ c New traffic lights ahead
❍ d Traffic lights out of order

Q343

These markings mean you are approaching

Mark one answer

- ❍ a a bus stop
- ❍ b a pedestrian crossing
- ❍ c a box junction
- ❍ d a parking zone

Q344

What does this sign mean?

Mark one answer

- ❍ a Waiting permitted
- ❍ b National speed limit applies
- ❍ c Waiting restrictions apply
- ❍ d Clearway – no stopping

Q345

A police car is following you. The police officer flashes the headlights and points to the left. What should you do?

Mark one answer

- ❍ a Pull up on the left
- ❍ b Turn next left
- ❍ c Stop immediately
- ❍ d Move over to the left

Q346

A red traffic light means

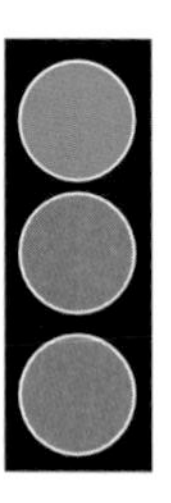

Mark one answer

- ❍ a you may drive straight on if there is no other traffic
- ❍ b you may turn left if it is safe to do so
- ❍ c you must stop behind the white stop line
- ❍ d you must slow down and prepare to stop if traffic has started to cross

Q347

You are waiting at a T-junction. A vehicle is coming from the right with the left signal flashing. What should you do?

Mark one answer

- ❍ a Move out and accelerate hard
- ❍ b Pull out before the vehicle reaches the junction
- ❍ c Wait until the vehicle starts to turn in
- ❍ d Move out slowly

Q348

What are triangular signs for?

Mark one answer

- ❍ a To give information
- ❍ b To give orders
- ❍ c To give directions
- ❍ d To give warnings

Q349

You want to stop just after a side road to the left. How should you signal?

Mark one answer

- ❍ a Wait until you have passed the junction, then signal left
- ❍ b Give a slowing-down arm signal before the junction
- ❍ c Give no signal at all
- ❍ d Signal left before the junction

Q350

What does this sign mean?

Mark one answer

- ❍ a You have priority
- ❍ b No overtaking
- ❍ c No motor vehicles
- ❍ d Two-way traffic

Q351

At traffic lights, amber on its own means

Mark one answer

- ❍ a prepare to go
- ❍ b stop at the stop line
- ❍ c go if the way is clear
- ❍ d go if no pedestrians are crossing

Q352

You MUST obey signs giving orders. These signs are mostly in

Mark one answer

- ❍ a green rectangles
- ❍ b red triangles
- ❍ c red circles
- ❍ d blue rectangles

Q353

What does this sign mean?

Mark one answer

- ❍ a Railway station
- ❍ b Route for cyclists
- ❍ c Scenic route
- ❍ d Ring road

Q354

What does this sign mean?

Mark one answer

- ❍ a Oncoming cars have priority
- ❍ b Two-way traffic
- ❍ c Do not overtake
- ❍ d No right turn ahead

Q355

What does this sign mean?

Mark one answer

- ❍ a Two-way traffic ahead across a one-way street
- ❍ b Traffic approaching you has priority
- ❍ c Motorway contraflow system ahead
- ❍ d Two-way traffic straight ahead

Q356

What does this sign mean?

Mark one answer

- ❍ a School-crossing patrol
- ❍ b No pedestrians allowed
- ❍ c Pedestrian crossing ahead
- ❍ d Pedestrian zone – no vehicle

Q357

How should you give an arm signal to turn LEFT?

Mark one answer

❍ a

❍ b

❍ c

❍ d

Q358

What does this motorway sign mean?

Mark one answer

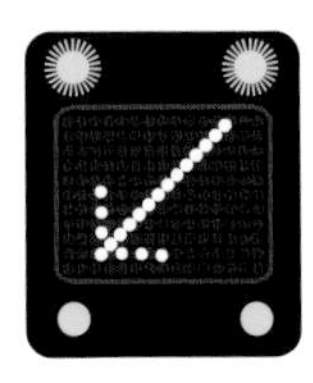

- ❍ a Leave the motorway at the next exit
- ❍ b Change to the opposite carriageway
- ❍ c Change to the lane on your left
- ❍ d Pull up on the hard shoulder

Q359

Which of these signs means there is a series of bends ahead?

Mark one answer

❍ a

❍ b

❍ c

❍ d

Q360

You see this sign ahead. It means

Mark one answer

❍ a national speed limit applies
❍ b no stopping
❍ c waiting restrictions
❍ d no entry

Q361

What does this sign mean?

Mark one answer

❍ a You are approaching a cycle route
❍ b Cyclists must dismount
❍ c Bicycles are not allowed
❍ d Walking is not allowed

Q362

Which of these signs warns you of a pedestrian crossing?

Mark one answer

❍ a

❍ b

❍ c

❍ d

Q363

Which arm signal tells a following vehicle you intend to turn left?

Mark one answer

❍ a

❍ b

❍ c

❍ d

Q364

You are approaching traffic lights. Red and amber are showing. This means

Mark one answer

- ❍ a pass the lights if the road is clear
- ❍ b wait for the green light before you pass the lights
- ❍ c there is a fault with the lights – take care
- ❍ d the lights are about to change to red

Q365

You see this line across the road at a roundabout. What does this mean?

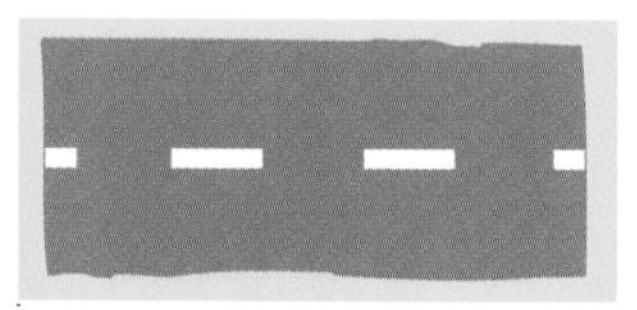

Mark one answer

- ❍ a Traffic from the left has right of way
- ❍ b You have right of way
- ❍ c Stop at the line
- ❍ d Give way to traffic from the right

Q366

What does this sign mean?

Mark one answer

- ❍ a Route for lorries
- ❍ b Rest area
- ❍ c Roundabout
- ❍ d Ring road

Q367

A red traffic light means

Mark one answer

- ❍ a you should stop unless turning left
- ❍ b stop if you are able to brake safely
- ❍ c you must stop and wait behind the stop line
- ❍ d proceed with caution

Q368

What does this sign mean?

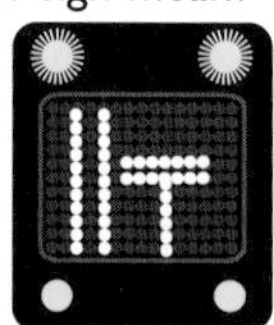

Mark one answer

- ❍ a Through traffic use left lane
- ❍ b Right-hand lane T-junction only
- ❍ c Right-hand lane closed ahead
- ❍ d 11-ton weight limit

Q369

You are approaching a red traffic light. The signal will change from red to

Mark one answer

- ❍ a green then amber
- ❍ b amber then green
- ❍ c red and amber then green
- ❍ d green and amber then green

Q370

Traffic signs giving orders are generally which shape?

Mark one answer

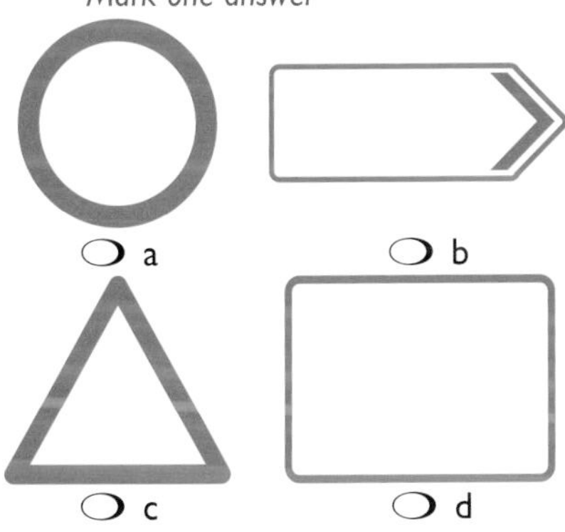

- ❍ a
- ❍ b
- ❍ c
- ❍ d

Q371

A white line like this along the centre of the road is a

Mark one answer

- ❍ a bus lane marking
- ❍ b hazard warning
- ❍ c give way marking
- ❍ d lane marking

Q372

Which sign means no overtaking?

Mark one answer

- ❍ a
- ❍ b
- ❍ c
- ❍ d

Q373

You are at a junction controlled by traffic lights. When should you NOT proceed at green?

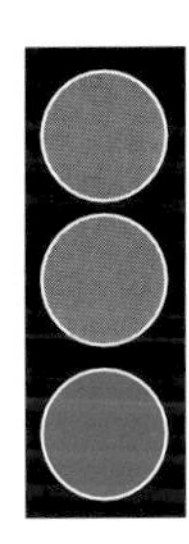

Mark one answer

- ❍ a When pedestrians are waiting to cross
- ❍ b When your exit from the junction is blocked
- ❍ c When you think the lights may be about to change
- ❍ d When you intend to turn right

Q374

When may you NOT overtake on the left?

Mark one answer

- ❍ a When the traffic is moving slowly in queues
- ❍ b On a one-way street
- ❍ c When the car in front is signalling to turn right
- ❍ d On a free-flowing motorway or dual carriageway

Q375

When may you sound the horn on your vehicle?

Mark one answer

- ❍ a To attract a friend's attention
- ❍ b To give you right of way
- ❍ c To make slower drivers move over
- ❍ d To warn other drivers of your presence

Q376

Which FOUR of these would be indicated by a triangular sign?

Mark four answer

- ❍ a Road narrows
- ❍ b Low bridge
- ❍ c Ahead only
- ❍ d Minimum speed
- ❍ e Children crossing
- ❍ f T-junction

Q377

A pelican crossing shows the flashing green man signal. What signal do drivers see?

Mark one answer

- ❍ a Red and amber
- ❍ b Flashing amber
- ❍ c Red
- ❍ d Flashing green

Q378

What does this sign mean?

Mark one answer

- ❍ a Road noise
- ❍ b Crosswinds
- ❍ c Airport
- ❍ d Adverse camber

Q379

How will a police officer in a patrol vehicle get you to stop?

Mark one answer

- ❍ a Flash the headlights, indicate left and point to the left
- ❍ b Wait until you stop then approach you
- ❍ c Use the siren, overtake then cut in front and stop
- ❍ d Pull alongside you, use the siren and wave you to stop

Q380

What does this sign mean?

Mark one answer

- a No overtaking
- b No motor vehicles
- c Clearway – no stopping
- d Cars and motorcycles only

Q381

What does this sign mean?

Mark one answer

- a The right-hand lane ahead is narrow
- b Right-hand lane for buses only
- c The right-hand lane is closed
- d No turning to the right

Q382

What does this traffic sign mean?

Mark one answer

- a No overtaking allowed
- b No U-turns allowed
- c One-way traffic only
- d Give priority to oncoming traffic

Q383

What does this motorway sign mean?

Mark one answer

- a Temporary minimum speed 50mph
- b No services for 50 miles
- c Obstruction 50 metres ahead
- d Temporary maximum speed 50mph

Q384

What does a sign with a brown background show?

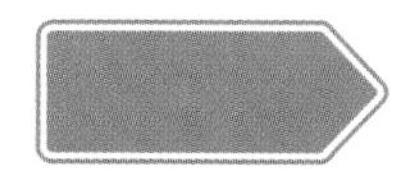

Mark one answer

- a Primary roads
- b Motorway routes
- c Tourist directions
- d Minor routes

Q385

You approach a junction. The traffic lights are not working. A police officer gives this signal. You should

Mark one answer

- a turn left only
- b turn right only
- c stop at the stop line
- d stop level with the officer's arm

Q386

On a motorway this sign means

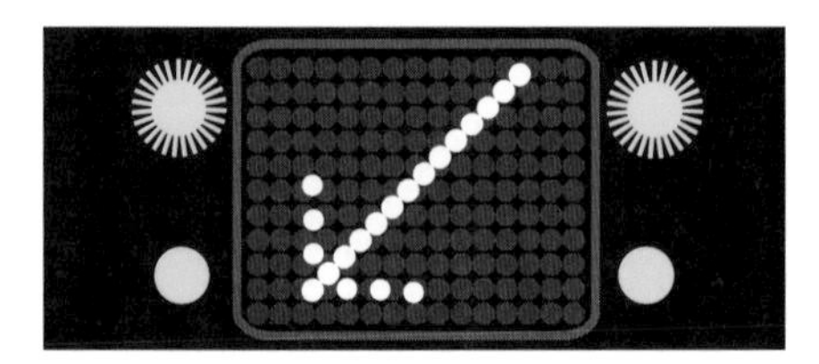

Mark one answer

- ❍ a move to the lane on your left
- ❍ b mover over onto the hard shoulder
- ❍ c pass a temporary obstruction on the left
- ❍ d leave the motorway at the next exit

Q387

You see this traffic light ahead. Which light(s) will come on next?

Mark one answer

- ❍ a Red and amber together
- ❍ b Green and amber together
- ❍ c Green alone
- ❍ d Red alone

Q388

What does this road marking mean?

Mark one answer

- ❍ a You are approaching a hazard
- ❍ b Do not cross the line
- ❍ c No stopping allowed
- ❍ d No overtaking allowed

Q389

What does this sign mean?

Mark one answer

- ❍ a No footpath ahead
- ❍ b Pedestrian crossing ahead
- ❍ c Pedestrians only ahead
- ❍ d School-crossing ahead

Answers and Explanations

Q321 b Red studs separate the hard shoulder from the left-hand lane. White studs mark the motorway lanes and green studs mark entrance and exit lanes.

Q322 b Red triangles usually give a warning.

Q323 a Red circles give orders.

Q324 a Then park in a safe place and check the indicators.

Q325 d Because the major road is on a bend your vision is restricted to both left and right.

Q326 a Red circles tell you what you must not do. Blue circles tell you what you must do. Rectangles usually give you information.

Q327 a

Q328 a, e & f It is the words 'legally authorised' that make this answer correct.

Q329 c

Q330 c 'c' is the correct answer because that is what flashing your headlights is supposed to mean. Not everyone knows or obeys the rules and may flash their headlights for other reasons, so always try to make sure of what they mean before you decide on any action.

Q331 d You must always stop at a stop sign.

Q332 a 'c' means no motor vehicles except motorcycles without sidecars.

Q333 b

Q334 d

Q335 b Circular signs with blue backgrounds tell you what you must do.

Q336 a

Q337 b Long lines with short gaps between them in the middle of the road are hazard warning lines. The more paint the more danger.

Q338 b

Q339 d You must go no further in that lane. You may change lanes and proceed, unless flashing red lights appear above all of them.

Q340 a This sign means no vehicles except bicycles being pushed by hand.

Q341 b

Q342 d

Q343 b

Q344 c There will also be a plate indicating when the restriction applies.

Q345 a You must stop, but 'c' is wrong because it may not be safe to stop immediately.

Q346 c You must always stop at a red traffic light.

Q347 c You need to be sure that the vehicle is really turning left before you pull out.

Q348 d

Q349 a The point of this question is that if you signal too early you may confuse people who will think you are turning left into the side road. There are times when 'b' would be useful, but you would also need to signal at an appropriate moment.

Q350 b
Q351 b An amber light means stop, and the lights will next change to red.
Q352 c
Q353 d
Q354 c
Q355 d
Q356 c
Q357 a
Q358 c Obviously you must make sure it is safe before doing so.
Q359 a
Q360 b This is a clearway sign and you must not stop at all.
Q361 a
Q362 a
Q363 c
Q364 b The next light will be green and you must wait to drive on until it appears.
Q365 d
Q366 d
Q367 c
Q368 c Always look well ahead and you will have plenty of time to react.
Q369 c The sequence of traffic lights is red, then red and amber, then green, then amber alone, then red.
Q370 a
Q371 b
Q372 a
Q373 b But also watch for other traffic.
Q374 d You must not overtake on the left on a motorway, or dual-carriageway, unless you are moving in queues of slow-moving traffic.
Q375 d Sounding your horn has the same meaning as flashing your headlights – to warn of your presence.
Q376 a, b, e & f All four of these are warnings of possible danger ahead.
Q377 b
Q378 b
Q379 a
Q380 b
Q381 c
Q382 d
Q383 d
Q384 c
Q385 c
Q386 a
Q387 d
Q388 a
Q389 b

Documents

Q390

Select TWO answers. To supervise a learner driver you MUST

Mark two answers

- ❍ a have held a full licence for at least 3 years
- ❍ b be an approved driving instructor
- ❍ c hold an advanced driving certificate
- ❍ d be at least 21

Q391

Which THREE pieces of information are found on a vehicle registration document?

Mark three answers

- ❍ a Registered keeper
- ❍ b Make of vehicle
- ❍ c Service history details
- ❍ d Date of MOT
- ❍ e Engine size
- ❍ f Type of insurance cover

Q392

Who MUST you show your driving licence to, on demand?

Mark one answer

- ❍ a A third party after an accident
- ❍ b A vehicle inspector
- ❍ c A uniformed police officer
- ❍ d A traffic warden

Q393

Motorcars and motorcycles must FIRST have an MOT test certificate when they are

Mark one answer

- ❍ a 1 year old
- ❍ b 3 years old
- ❍ c 5 years old
- ❍ d 7 years old

Q394

What should you bring with you when taking your driving test?

Mark one answer

- ❍ a A service record book
- ❍ b An insurance certificate
- ❍ c A signed driving licence
- ❍ d An MOT certificate

Q395

What is the legal minimum insurance cover you must have to drive on public roads?

Mark one answer

- ❍ a Third party only
- ❍ b Third party fire and theft
- ❍ c Fully comprehensive
- ❍ d Personal injury cover

Q396

A police officer asks to see your driving documents. You don't have them with you. You must produce them at a police station within

Mark one answer

- a 5 days
- b 7 days
- c 21 days
- d 14 days

Q397

To drive on the road, learners MUST

Mark one answer

- a have a signed, valid provisional licence
- b have NO penalty points on their licence
- c have taken professional instruction
- d apply for a driving test within 12 months

Q398

Which THREE of the following do you need before you can drive legally?

Mark three answers

- a Proof of identity
- b A signed driving licence
- c Fully comprehensive insurance
- d A vehicle handbook
- e A valid tax disk displayed on your vehicle
- f A current MOT certificate if the car is over three years old

Q399

Before driving anyone else's motor vehicle you should make sure that

Mark one answer

- a the vehicle is insured for your use
- b the vehicle owner has third party insurance cover
- c your own vehicle has insurance cover
- d the owner has left the insurance documents in the vehicle

Q400

For which TWO of these must you show your motor insurance certificate?

Mark two answers

- a When a police officer asks you for them
- b When you are taking your driving test
- c When buying or selling a vehicle
- d When you are taxing your vehicle
- e When having an MOT inspection

Q401

When is it legal to drive a car over three years old without an MOT certificate?

Mark one answer

- a Up to seven days after the old certificate has run out
- b When driving to an appointment at an MOT centre
- c When driving to an MOT centre to arrange an appointment
- d Just after buying a second-hand car with no MOT

Answers and Explanations

Q390 **a & d** You must be at least 21 years of age, and the licence you have held for three years must still be valid and be for the category of vehicle being driven.

Q391 **a, b & e**

Q392 **c**

Q393 **b**

Q394 **c**

Q395 **a** This only covers damage to other people and their property.

Q396 **b** You may select the police station of your choice.

Q397 **a** You are not allowed to drive until you have applied for and received your provisional licence and have signed it in ink.

Q398 **b, e & f** 'c' does not apply because it says fully comprehensive insurance.

Q399 **a** Your own vehicle insurance may cover you as a passenger in another person's vehicle but very rarely covers you to drive it.

Q400 **a & d**

Q401 **b** If your car is over three years old and has no valid MOT certificate, you must pre-book an appointment at an MOT centre before you drive it there.

Driving Theory Test Questions

Accident Handling

Q402

When are you allowed to use hazard warning lights?

Mark one answer

❍ a When driving during darkness without headlights
❍ b When parked for shopping on double yellow lines
❍ c When stopped and temporarily obstructing traffic
❍ d When travelling slowly because you are lost

Q403

For which TWO should you use hazard warning lights?

Mark two answers

❍ a When you wish to stop on double yellow lines
❍ b When you slow down quickly on a motorway because of a hazard ahead
❍ c When you need to park on the pavement
❍ d When you have broken down

Q404

You have an accident while driving and someone else is injured. You do not produce your insurance certificate when requested at the time. You must report it to the police as soon as possible, or in any case within

Mark one answer

❍ a 24 hours
❍ b 48 hours
❍ c 5 days
❍ d 7 days

Q405

You are in an accident on an A-class road. At what distance before the obstruction should you place a warning triangle?

Mark one answer

❍ a 25 metres (80 feet)
❍ b 50 metres (165 feet)
❍ c 100 metres (330 feet)
❍ d 150 metres (495 feet)

Q406

You break down on a level crossing. The lights have not yet begun to flash. Which THREE things should you do?

Mark three answers

❍ a Walk down the track and signal the next train
❍ b Telephone the signal operator
❍ c Leave your vehicle and get everyone clear
❍ d Move the vehicle if a signal operator tells you to
❍ e Tell drivers behind what has happened

Q407

You are involved in an accident. A passenger in another vehicle is slightly injured. Do you have to report it to the police?

Mark one answer

❍ a Yes, you must report it within 28 days
❍ b No, the injured passenger should decide whether to report it
❍ c No, slight injuries should not involve the police
❍ d Yes, you must report it to the police as soon as possible

Q408

You are travelling on a motorway.
A suitcase falls from your vehicle.
There are valuables in the suitcase.
What should you do?

Mark one answer

- ❍ a Reverse your vehicle carefully and collect the case as quickly as possible
- ❍ b Stop wherever you are and pick up the case but only when there is a safe gap
- ❍ c Stop on the hard shoulder and then retrieve the suitcase yourself
- ❍ d Stop on the hard shoulder and use the emergency telephone to inform the police

Q409

Your vehicle is broken down on a straight road. Where should you place a warning triangle?

Mark one answer

- ❍ a Securely on the roof of your vehicle
- ❍ b 10 metres (11 yards) from your vehicle
- ❍ c 50 metres (55 yards) from your vehicle
- ❍ d Directly at the rear of your vehicle

Q410

What safeguard could you take against fire risk to your vehicle?

Mark one answer

- ❍ a Keep water levels above maximum
- ❍ b Avoid driving with a full tank of fuel
- ❍ c Use unleaded petrol
- ❍ d Check out any strong smell of petrol

Q411

At a railway level crossing, the red light signal continues to flash after a train has gone by. What should you do?

Mark one answer

- ❍ a Phone the signal operator
- ❍ b Wait
- ❍ c Alert drivers behind you
- ❍ d Proceed with caution

Q412

Your vehicle has broken down on an automatic railway level crossing.
What should you do FIRST?

Mark one answer

- ❍ a Phone the signal operator so that trains can be stopped
- ❍ b Walk along the track to give warning to any approaching trains
- ❍ c Try to push the vehicle clear of the crossing as soon as possible
- ❍ d Get everyone out of the vehicle and clear of the crossing

Q413

Your tyre bursts while you are driving. Which TWO should you do?

Mark two answers

❍ a Select reverse gear to stop the vehicle
❍ b Give a stopping arm signal and use the gears to slow down
❍ c Pull up slowly at the side of the road
❍ d Stop the vehicle by braking as quickly as possible
❍ e Hold the steering wheel firmly to keep control

Q414

Which TWO things should you do when a front tyre bursts?

Mark two answers

❍ a Change down and brake hard
❍ b Let the vehicle roll to a stop
❍ c Brake firmly and quickly
❍ d Grip the steering wheel firmly
❍ e Hold the steering wheel lightly

Q415

Your vehicle breaks down on a motorway. You go to the emergency telephone. Your passenger should

Mark one answer

❍ a wait on the embankment away from the hard shoulder
❍ b stand next to the vehicle on the hard shoulder
❍ c accompany you to the telephone
❍ d wait inside the vehicle

Q416

For which THREE should you use your hazard warning lights?

Mark three answers

❍ a When you are temporarily obstructing traffic
❍ b To warn following traffic of a hazard ahead
❍ c When you are parking in a restricted area
❍ d When you have broken down

Q417

You have broken down on a two-way road. You should place a warning triangle at least how far from your vehicle?

Mark one answer

❍ a 5 metres (5 yards)
❍ b 25 metres (27 yards)
❍ c 50 metres (55 yards)
❍ d 100 metres (110 yards)

Q418

Your vehicle has a puncture on a motorway. What should you do?

Mark one answer

- ❍ a Drive slowly to the next service area to get assistance
- ❍ b Pull up on the hard shoulder. Change the wheel as quickly as possible
- ❍ c Pull up on the hard shoulder. Use the emergency phone to get assistance
- ❍ d Switch on you hazard lights. Stop in your lane

Q419

You have stopped at the scene of an accident to give help. Which THREE things should you do?

Mark three answers

- ❍ a Keep injured people on the move by walking them around
- ❍ b Give injured people a warm drink
- ❍ c Keep injured people warm and comfortable
- ❍ d Keep injured people calm by talking to them reassuringly
- ❍ e Make sure injured people are not left alone

Q420

You are the first to arrive at the scene of an accident. Which FOUR of these should you do?

Mark four answers

- ❍ a Switch off the vehicle engines
- ❍ b Leave as soon as another motorist arrives
- ❍ c Move uninjured people away from the vehicles
- ❍ d Call the emergency services
- ❍ e Warn other traffic

Q421

You break down on an ordinary road. Your warning triangle should be displayed

Mark one answer

- ❍ a on the roof of your vehicle
- ❍ b just behind your vehicle
- ❍ c at least 50 metres (55 yards) behind your vehicle
- ❍ d at least 150 metres (164 yards) behind your vehicle

Q422

You have stalled in the middle of a level crossing and cannot re-start the engine. The warning bell starts to ring. You should

Mark one answer

❍ a run down the track to warn the signalman
❍ b get out and clear of the crossing
❍ c carry on trying to re-start the engine
❍ d push the vehicle clear of the crossing

Q423

You arrive at the scene of an accident involving a lorry carrying dangerous chemicals. What should you do before you dial 999?

Mark one answer

❍ a Try to move the lorry
❍ b Try to dilute the chemicals by washing them away with water
❍ c Find out about the chemicals from labels on the lorry
❍ d Try to stop the chemicals spreading

Q424

When should you switch on your hazard warning lights?

Mark one answer

❍ a When you are driving slowly due to bad weather
❍ b When you are towing a broken-down vehicle
❍ c When you are parked on double yellow lines
❍ d When you cannot avoid causing an obstruction

Q425

You are on the motorway. Luggage falls from your vehicle. What should you do?

Mark one answer

❍ a Stop on the motorway and put on hazard lights while you pick it up
❍ b Reverse back up the motorway to pick it up
❍ c Stop at the next emergency telephone and contact the police
❍ d Pull up on the hard shoulder and wave traffic down

Q426

You arrive at the scene of a motorcycle accident. The rider is conscious but in shock. You should make sure that

Mark one answer

❍ a the rider's helmet is removed
❍ b the rider's helmet is not removed
❍ c the rider is moved to the side of the road
❍ d the rider is put in the recovery position

Q427

You are driving on a motorway. A large box falls onto the carriageway from a lorry ahead of you. The lorry does not stop. You should

Mark one answer

❍ a catch up with the lorry and try to get the driver's attention
❍ b stop close to the box and switch on your hazard warning lights until the police arrive
❍ c pull over to the hard shoulder then try to remove the box
❍ d drive to the next emergency telephone and inform the police

Q428

You are the first person to arrive at an accident where people are badly injured. Which THREE should you do?

Mark three answers

❍ a Switch on your own hazard warning lights
❍ b Make sure someone telephones for an ambulance
❍ c Try and get people who are injured to drink something
❍ d Move the people who are injured clear of their vehicles
❍ e Get people who are not injured clear of the scene

Q429

A tanker is involved in an accident. Which sign would show if the tanker is carrying dangerous goods?

Mark one answer

❍ a

LONG VEHICLE

❍ b

❍ c

❍ d

Answers and Explanations

Q402 **c**
Q403 **b & d**
Q404 **a** Note that you have 24 hours in which to report the accident but are allowed up to seven days in which to produce your driving licence, insurance and MOT certificates if required to do so.
Q405 **b** 50 metres is recommended on A-roads and 150 metres on motorways and dual-carriageways.
Q406 **b, c & d**
Q407 **d** Any accident involving injury to another person must be reported to the police as soon as possible and within 24 hours.
Q408 **d** This is the only safe option as 'a', 'b' and 'c' are all highly dangerous.
Q409 **c**
Q410 **d**
Q411 **b** This usually means another train is coming.
Q412 **d** Your first action is to get everyone to safety. Other actions can follow.
Q413 **c & e** You will need both hands firmly on the wheel in order to control the car, and using the gears or brakes is likely to make your car swerve. When possible it is safest just to let your car roll to a halt at the side of the road.
Q414 **b & d**
Q415 **a** This is where your passengers are safest and well away from other traffic.
Q416 **a, b & d** The fact that you are obstructing other traffic should be unintentional and unavoidable for 'a' to be correct.
Q417 **c**
Q418 **c** The hard shoulder of a motorway is a dangerous place and 'c' is the safest course of action. It can be particularly dangerous to try to change an offside wheel as you may be very close to fast-moving traffic in the left-hand lane.
Q419 **c, d & e** You should not move injured people unless they are in danger; nor should you give them anything to drink.
Q420 **a, c, d & e**
Q421 **c**
Q422 **b** A train may arrive within seconds so 'b' is the only safe possibility.
Q423 **c** Remember to keep your distance and look for an orange label on the side or rear of the vehicle. It will show details of the load being carried.
Q424 **d**
Q425 **c**
Q426 **b** The helmet is giving support in the case of head injury.
Q427 **d**
Q428 **a, b & e**
Q429 **a**

Driving Theory Test Questions

Vehicle Loading

Q430

Who is responsible for making sure a vehicle is not overloaded?

Mark one answer

❍ a The driver of the vehicle
❍ b The owner of the items being carried
❍ c The person who loaded the vehicle
❍ d The owner of the vehicle

Q431

Would it be safe to allow children to sit BEHIND the rear seats of a hatchback car?

Mark one answer

❍ a No, not in any circumstances
❍ b Yes, if you can see clearly to the rear
❍ c Yes, if they are under 11 years
❍ d No, unless all the other seats are full

Q432

If a trailer swerves or snakes when you are towing it, you should

Mark one answer

❍ a let go of the steering wheel and let it correct itself
❍ b brake hard and hold the pedal down
❍ c increase your speed as quickly as possible
❍ d ease off the accelerator and reduce your speed

Q433

Any load that is carried on a roof rack MUST be

Mark one answer

❍ a carried only when strictly necessary
❍ b as light as possible
❍ c covered with plastic sheeting
❍ d securely fastened when driving

Q434

What do child locks in a vehicle do?

Mark one answer

❍ a Lock the seat belt buckles in place
❍ b Stop children from opening rear doors
❍ c Lock the rear windows in the up position
❍ d Stop the rear seats from tipping forwards

Q435

How can you stop a caravan snaking from side to side?

Mark one answer

❍ a Turn the steering wheel slowly to each side
❍ b Accelerate to increase your speed
❍ c Slow down very gradually
❍ d Stop as quickly as you can

Q436

Which THREE are suitable restraints for a child under three years?

Mark one answer

- ❍ a A child seat
- ❍ b An adult holding a child
- ❍ c An adult seat belt
- ❍ d A lap belt
- ❍ e A harness
- ❍ f A baby carrier

Q437

You should load a trailer so that the weight is

Mark one answer

- ❍ a mostly over the nearside wheel
- ❍ b evenly distributed
- ❍ c mainly at the front
- ❍ d mostly at the rear

Q438

You are towing a caravan along a motorway. The caravan begins to swerve from side to side. What should you do?

Mark one answer

- ❍ a Steer sharply from side to side
- ❍ b Do an emergency stop
- ❍ c Speed up a little
- ❍ d Ease off the accelerator slowly

Q439

When would it be safe for children to sit behind the rear seats in a hatchback car?

Mark one answer

- ❍ a On short journeys
- ❍ b On minor roads
- ❍ c Never
- ❍ d At any time

Answers and Explanations

Q430 **a**

Q431 **a** The area behind the rear seats of a hatchback car is designed to crumple in the event of a collision and is therefore not a safe place to sit.

Q432 **d** 'a', 'b' and 'c' would all be likely to make the problem worse.

Q433 **d** The word 'MUST' in the question makes 'd' correct, but 'a' and 'b' are recommended.

Q434 **b** Child locks prevent the rear doors being opened from the inside.

Q435 **c**

Q436 **a, e & f**

Q437 **b** This creates the greatest stability.

Q438 **d**

Q439 **c**

BSM